I Corinthians
FOR BEGINNERS

MIKE MAZZALONGO

THE "FOR BEGINNERS" SERIES

The "For Beginners" series of video classes and books provide a non-technical and easy to understand presentation of Bible books and topics that are rich in information and application for the beginner as well as the mature Bible student.

For more information visit:|
bibletalk.tv/for-beginners

TABLE OF CONTENTS

INTRODUCTION

The Apostle Paul's first letter to the church in Corinth has long served as a source for practical spiritual advice to churches experiencing growing pains. In it Paul deals with all manner of conflict, bad behavior, spiritual immaturity and misunderstanding that was happening at the church in Corinth, and that many churches go through at various points in their development today.

This book groups together some of the major ideas covered in this comprehensive primer for normal church life. Each chapter develops a single theme and carries the reader through the entire epistle.

1.
THE FOOLISHNESS OF GOD

I CORINTHIANS 1:18-31

To have a better understanding of this and all the material to follow, it would be helpful to know a little background about this particular congregation, and why Paul wrote to them in the first place.

Corinth was the commercial center of Greece. It was four times larger and about fifty miles west of Athens. It had a population of 400,000 people making it the fourth largest and richest cities in the Roman Empire. It was also one of the wickedest. It was here in the years 52-53 AD that Paul established a church right in the shadow of Athenian philosophy. Athena was the patron of Athens; she was the goddess of wisdom, arts and crafts. It was believed that her wisdom created the cosmos.

After establishing this congregation and moving on to other works, a delegation from Corinth came to Paul with news of serious disputes and problems that had arisen in the Corinthian church. I Corinthians is one of several letters Paul wrote to this church in order to deal with its many problems. One of the main problems stemmed from the fact that this church was made up of mostly Greek (or Gentile) converts. Unlike the Jews who were well trained in moral living and religious worship to God, Greeks came from an extremely immoral sexual background and had many false ideas about God and religion. This had been planted in them by a long history of Greek philosophers and pagan religious teachers. Because of this, they had more difficulty in adapting to the Christian lifestyle than the Jews did. They were either slow in maturing or they tried to mesh their former pagan ideas and philosophies with the teachings and practices of Christ.

And so, the delegation from Corinth reported problems such as sexual immorality, poor conduct during worship, misuse of spiritual gifts and the very dangerous issue of divisiveness. In writing to them about all of these problems Paul tackles the issue of divisiveness first, seeing it as the most dangerous. If the church divides, there is no opportunity to work on the other issues because people are too filled with anger and resentment.

In verse 10 of the first chapter Paul says:

> Now, I exhort you, brethren, by the name of our Lord Jesus Christ that you all agree, and there be no divisions among you.

When we continue to read his letter, and if we know some of the habits of that culture, we learn the nature and cause of their division.

In those days various trained speakers called orators would develop a following by staking out a position on a philosophy or political idea and debate others on the merits of their position. It was this system that Paul encountered when he was in Athens, and invited to speak on Mars Hill.

These debaters would build up a following based on their skills in public speaking and formal debate. They were like verbal gladiators. The better they were, the bigger their following. This type of thing was beginning to happen in the church, with different teachers staking out positions that they claimed were endorsed by an Apostle or church leader. Some would say, "I am arguing the position of Peter," and another would say, "My position is consistent with Paul's teachings."

The Greek Christians in the church were adopting a familiar form of intellectual exercise to the practice of their faith in Christ.

In dealing with this problem, Paul states in verse 17 that his preaching was not based on "cleverness of speech." This was a direct reference to the debating style and practice beginning to take hold of Corinth.

Paul goes on to say that their system not only produced division, but it also made "void" or "empty" or "useless" the cross of Christ. His idea was that by relying on the power of persuasion and debate to convince men to believe, they took away the power of the cross of Christ to draw men to faith.

Paul shows how it is very tempting to use human methods to bring people to Christ because God's methods (preaching the cross) seems so foolish by comparison. In verses 18-31 he gives the Corinthians three reasons why God's way to save people seems foolish to human understanding.

The Message Itself is Foolish – vs. 18-25

Human beings through their own reasoning, schemes, plans, and philosophies have never been able to provide real hope for the world. No human system gives complete peace of mind and sure confidence in facing death. And, mankind has not been able, through its own efforts, to know the mind of God. Of course, this has not stopped one thinker after another to offer explanations and solutions to the mystery of life and death.

Paul explains to the Corinthians how God's plan and solution compares to all of theirs.

> Vs. 18-20 – For the word of the cross is foolishness to those who are perishing, but to us who are being saved it is the power of God. For it is written, "I will destroy the wisdom of the wise, and the cleverness of the clever I will set aside." Where is the wise man? Where is the scribe? Where is the debater of this age? Has not God made foolish the wisdom of the world?

God's message, that through the death of one, everyone else could have eternal life, seemed foolish. After all, what possible connection could the dying of a poor Jewish carpenter have to do with the life of a Greek businessman a thousand miles away? Of course, for the one who believed that this was no ordinary Jewish carpenter, but in fact the Son of God, His death and resurrection made a lot of sense and provided the message of hope they were looking for.

> Vs. 21-25 – For since in the wisdom of God the world through its wisdom did not come to know God, God was well pleased through the foolishness of the message preached to save those who believe. For indeed Jews ask for signs and Greeks search for wisdom; but we preach Christ crucified, to Jews a stumbling block and to Gentiles foolishness, but to those who are called, both Jews and Greeks, Christ the power of God and the wisdom of God. Because the foolishness of God is wiser than men, and the weakness of God is stronger than men.

The fact that the world considered this message nonsense was nothing new. The world has never understood God's message for the most part. Jews were not content to hear the word of prophecy fulfilled; they wanted spectacular signs and wonders in order to be convinced of Christ's identity. The Greeks wanted the mysteries explained; they searched for wisdom in human terms rather than the solution offered in Christ.

On the surface, to base your hope of eternal life and joy on the preaching and promises of a dead Jew, executed as a criminal, was pretty foolish. But Paul reminds them that for those who did believe, the wisdom and power of God would be fully revealed in Christ.

The Corinthians understood what he meant because their faith had been rewarded with great spiritual powers and gifts (i.e. tongues).

Paul lays out a great truth here for his readers:

- Faith comes before insight
- Believing precedes understanding
- Obedience first, rewards second

For those who accepted Jesus in faith and obedience, what seemed foolish to the world became, through experience and insight, the wisdom and power of God. These Corinthians believed that, then they saw the power of God working in their lives, not vice-versa.

The Messengers Were Foolish – Vs. 26-29

People who change the world try to do so with the same array of tools:

- Power – usually military

- Intelligence – new philosophy; new social systems

- Religion – prophets that come and go

In contrast, the messengers of the gospel and the recipients of the message (Apostles, disciples, and the Christians that follow throughout the ages) have no such credentials.

- Not many wise or great thinkers

- Not many powerful or rich

Paul says that God has deliberately chosen the weak, the lowly and the powerless to bring the message that ultimately changes people's lives in ways that no other "message" can. The messengers may seem foolish in the eyes of the world, but the results of their message in the lives of those who believe cannot be denied.

Their power and wisdom was a message to the world that God could take something weak, despised and foolish, and transform it into something powerful, holy and wise. This is something that great leaders in the world had failed to do with all of their abilities because of the method they used. And yet, they considered God's method foolish...

The Method Was Foolish – Vs. 30-31

> Vs. 30-31 – But by His doing you are in Christ Jesus, who became to us wisdom from God, and righteousness and sanctification, and redemption, so that, just as it is written, "Let him who boasts, boast in the Lord."

God's ways are not man's ways.

> How unsearchable are His judgments and unfathomable are His ways. - Romans 11:33

Man is either reasonable and logical, looking for the connections between everything; or, he is totally selfish and hedonistic, searching only for the pleasure and satisfaction something will bring. Humans fluctuate between these two extremes, and judge things in this context. God is spiritual. He does things on another plane, beyond human reasoning or feeling.

The method used by God to save man from the consequences of sin, which are guilt, shame, fear, suffering and ultimately death and condemnation, does not answer to man's reasoning or feelings. It isn't subject to logic; it is rather foolish by man's standards. The method is called "imputation" and the motivation is God's unconditional love.

Paul summarizes the idea of imputation in verse 30 by saying all the things we need to be in order to be saved from death:

- Knowledgeable – wise

- Acceptable – righteous

- Purified – sanctified

- Free from sin – redeemed

Jesus becomes all of these things for us, and through faith in Him these things are imputed or put upon us as if we truly possessed them, and thus become saved.

In other words, things that we as humans could never obtain through any method (like absolute purity, rightness with God, freedom from sin of any kind, knowledge of God, etc.) God gives to us freely because we are associated with Christ (in Christ) through faith.

Jesus obtains these by living a perfect human life, offering Himself in a sacrificial death and appearing after a miraculous resurrection. We, on the other hand, freely receive these blessings through faith, which is a response that humans can make. And God has devised this way of doing things because He continues to love those who hate and disobey Him.

Man would have never figured this out, and continues to laugh at this method as the solution to man's problems to this very day! The method seems foolish, but for those who are "in Christ" it is a solution for which they continually praise or "boast" in the Lord.

Summary

I think the greatest insult to me as an individual in this society is to be considered irrelevant. It seems that the "serious" people who are in charge of solving the problems of the world put preachers at the bottom of the list of those who might offer a solution to hate, fear, unhappiness and disorder. This is probably one of the main reasons why some do not go into ministry on a full time basis.

We are irrelevant, or "foolish," because:

- Our message requires belief in what is unseen.

- Our messengers are without influence, power or prestige.

- Our method demands the relinquishing of human effort in favor of total dependence on God.

And yet, for those that believe:

- The unseen has become real and powerful in their lives.

- The method has removed fear and guilt, and replaced it with hope, a sense of meaning and purpose in life.

- The converts themselves have become messengers for the foolish things of God, confounding the wise and powerful of this world.

I think that we should rejoice if we are considered foolish or irrelevant because this means that they have at least recognized us for who we truly are: Christians! Jesus says that we should rejoice if we are persecuted for being His disciples.

How does the world see you? Are you one of its own? Are you wise, strong, noble and relevant, or are you one of the foolish ones that believe in God's message and method preached by one of His messengers?

How will you resolve your fears, your judgment and your eternal life? Will you rely on yourself, ignore it or let the foolishness of God clothe you with forgiveness, salvation and eternal life?

If you believe in Jesus and God's work through Him, then you're one of the foolish ones, and your foolish faith will be rewarded.

2.
THE POWER OF THE CROSS

I CORINTHIANS 2:1-5

In the previous chapter we looked at how the Apostle Paul responded to those who were causing division in the church at Corinth. It seems that there were some who were cultivating a following by debating other teachers on various points of doctrine. They measured their success by the size of their audience and the eloquence of their preaching. In addition to this, they tried to bolster their reputations by aligning themselves with the Apostles or other great teachers, even Jesus Himself.

This, of course, was causing the church to break into camps, and shifting the focus of the church away from God and onto their preferred teachers, and this led to pride and division.

In chapter 2:1-5, Paul compares himself and his teaching to those men, and reveals the true source of power in the church, the cross of Jesus Christ.

> Vs. 1 – And when I came to you, brethren, I did not come with superiority of speech or of wisdom, proclaiming to you the testimony of God.

Paul still refers to them as brethren, even though their activities are sinful, immature and discouraging. He continues to extend the hand of fellowship, which is what contributes to unity and peace.

In comparing his "style" with theirs in preaching and teaching, he acknowledges that he is not a trained speaker, orator or philosopher as they were. This is not false modesty or irony; he is not saying this "tongue in cheek" to be sarcastic. Paul acknowledged that others did not find his public speaking ability very impressive (II Corinthians 10:10).

And so, by self-admittance, in the present competition between the various teachers based on style and appeal, he admits that he would not do well.

> Vs. 2 – For I determined to know nothing among you except Jesus Christ, and Him crucified.

In this verse, he also acknowledges that his ability or lack of it is not the point anyway; his original intent was to bring them the gospel of Jesus Christ, pure and simple.

The good news that Jesus, the Son of God, came in the form of a man, and lived among men for a time teaching, healing and doing miracles. How Jesus died in order to pay for the moral debt caused by the sins of all men. The good news that on the third day after His death, He was resurrected through the power of the Holy Spirit in order to prove that He was God, and that sin would now be forgiven and eternal life would now be offered through faith in Him. Paul said that his objective was not to impress anyone with his style; his objective was to bring to them this simple message of the gospel.

> Vs. 3 – I was with you in weakness and in fear and in much trembling.

He reminds them of the original circumstances of his preaching to them.

- He had just been ridiculed in Athens.
- He was near the end of a grueling mission trip.
- He was in an unfriendly pagan city with no church, only a few Christians and a tremendous job to do.

Unlike the Corinthian teachers who had a ready-made audience, Paul was constantly disputing with the Jews at the beginning of his ministry in Corinth.

> Vs. 4 – And my message and my preaching were not in persuasive words of wisdom, but in demonstration of the Spirit and of power,

Paul now makes the true comparison between his preaching and theirs, based on the criteria that really counted. He mentions the attributes of their preaching:

- Persuasiveness – logic, argument, style, debate, eloquence.
- Wisdom – refers to human intelligence, strategy, knowledge, training.

Then he compares this with the main elements of his preaching:

- Spirit – his message was a message from the Spirit of God, not some clever new philosophy or argument designed by man.
- Power – the power of God also accompanied his message. They simply had to look at the miraculous gifts they now possessed to confirm that the power of God was at work among them.

Each of their preaching styles had certain elements, but Paul demonstrates that his preaching came from God and this fact was confirmed by the power of God. He doesn't state it, but the obvious conclusion is that his preaching (although not as eloquent) was much more dynamic and important, and much more powerful in its results.

> Vs. 5 – so that your faith would not rest on the wisdom of men, but on the power of God.

Now, just in case they might think that he is playing the same game that they are, he quickly reminds them why his preaching is so much more effective than theirs.

The object of the preaching is faith in God, and through Paul's preaching men believed in God because of what God did, not what Paul did. Paul understood that the power of God was not demonstrated by the tongues of men but rather by the cross of Christ. His preaching was superior because it revealed the power of the cross of Jesus Christ, which among other things had the power to do three things.

The preaching of the cross had the power to destroy Satan and death.

> Therefore, since the children share in flesh and blood, He Himself likewise also partook of the same, that through death He might render powerless him who had the

> power of death, that is, the devil, and might free those who through fear of death were subject to slavery all their lives.
> - Hebrews 2:14-15

Through His death and resurrection, Jesus removed from Satan the ability to lead men into sin without hope of forgiveness, thus leading to death.

Before the cross there was no real way to pay for sin, so whomever Satan seduced into sin was doomed to be condemned and suffer eternally.

With the cross of Jesus, God pays the debt for sin so that even if men continue to sin there is now a way to cleanse them and avoid eternal damnation.

Satan doesn't lose his ability to deceive and seduce, but he no longer can do eternal damage to our souls. He is thus defeated, and so is death.

There is an "antidote" to the deadly infection of sin – the cross of Christ.

The preaching of the cross has the power to create hope.

In Colossians 1:5 Paul talks about the "..hope which is laid up in heaven, of which you previously heard in the word of truth, the gospel."

Before the cross of Jesus, people could only speculate about life after death. Those who had some spiritual insight understood that there was some relationship with the way that a person acted here on earth and what would happen later. In pagan religions people would try all manner of sacrifice (even sacrificing their own children) in an attempt to appease the gods. Others would build elaborate burial places in preparation to enter another world that they thought was much like this one.

The cross, however, provides real hope for man's guilty conscience before God, as well as a demonstration of God's willingness to resurrect man from the grave. Unlike the promises of men that are not always kept under the best of circumstances, the preaching of the cross produces hope because God never fails in carrying out His promises.

The preaching of the cross has the power to draw all men to God.

Jesus said,

> "And I, if I am lifted up from the earth, will draw all men to myself." John 12:32

Jesus said this to his apostles to indicate the manner that He would die: crucifixion. I am impressed by the word "all" in this verse because it says that everyone will or can be drawn by the cross of Jesus. I don't think Jesus meant that all people would be fascinated by crucifixion as a manner of dying. I think Jesus meant that what He was doing was on behalf of all people since all people needed it, and all people would recognize their universal need for forgiveness and His way of offering it to them.

Throughout history missionaries have not had problems with different cultures and languages responding to the cross so long as they can explain it in their own language; the heart is always drawn to the cross once the head understands the message.

Summary

Paul reminds the Corinthians that the power of salvation is the gospel, not the gospel preachers; and the power of the gospel is the power of the cross. The cross has the power:

A. To destroy Satan and death because it provides an antidote to the poison of sin that Satan seduces us into, causing our spiritual death. We're guilty of sin but the cross provides the forgiveness and healing we need.

B. To create hope in one's heart by demonstrating God's power. I can have a secure expectation that all my sins are forgiven, and I will be resurrected to eternal life because of the power I see operating in Jesus' death and resurrection. If God can do that for Jesus, He can surely do this for me.

C. To draw everyone to God. Sin is universal and affects everyone the same way (death) regardless of time or culture. The cross is also universal because everyone can understand the meaning of it for their own lives. Forgiveness, reconciliation, life after death – these are all universal experiences that are beyond culture or time (i.e. the parable of the prodigal son is as clearly understood today in our internet world as it was in first century Israel).

One of the points that we need to take away from this lesson is that the power is in the gospel message – not in the messenger. You sharing your faith, your story of conversion, the details of the gospel over lunch with a friend, is as powerful as the minister preaching a prepared sermon from the pulpit. The reason for this is that the power to change hearts from disbelief to belief and the power to draw men closer to God resides in the message – not the messenger.

The only way to reach the lost is to find ways to repeat the message to as many people and as many times as possible. This is why we say that the goal of our BibleTalk.tv ministry is to preach the gospel to the world every day without fail until Jesus returns.

3.
TOP TEN THINGS THAT KILL GROWTH

I CORINTHIANS 2:1-6:20

The church at Corinth had a lot of things going for it that promoted growth:

- Good location in a key city

- No other congregation there

- Established by an Apostle (credibility, sound teaching)

- Many talented people who possessed "spiritual gifts"

Even though it had these advantages, I don't think it was a growing church because it didn't seem to be practicing the things that make for church growth. Not only this, but as we read chapters 2-6 we notice that Paul lists ten things that they were doing that were actually killing the growth of the church.

1. Second Guessing God

> Vs. 12-14 – Now we have received, not the spirit of the world, but the Spirit who is from God, so that we may know the things freely given to us by God, which things we also speak, not in words taught by human wisdom, but in those taught by the Spirit, combining spiritual thoughts with spiritual words.

The very first and deadly attack that Satan tried, and continues to try today, is to make believers doubt – not the power or the person of God – but doubt that His word is His word or that it has authority (i.e. Eve, King Saul, even Jesus were tempted to disregard the word).

The basis of our personal and corporate growth as the church is directly related to our acceptance and obedience of God's word (Jesus said "Teaching them to obey all that I have commanded" - Matthew 28:20).

2. Being Big Babies

> 3:1-3 – And I, brethren, could not speak to you as to spiritual men, but as to men of flesh, as to infants in Christ. I gave you milk to drink, not solid food; for you were not yet able to receive it. Indeed, even now you are not yet able, for you are still fleshly. For since there is jealousy and strife among you, are you not fleshly, and are you not walking like mere men?

They had a good start but they refused to move on from that point.

Immaturity isn't just being "young" or new in Christ, it is the refusal to grow in one's faith. Some people have been in the church for twenty years but are not any different, don't do any more, don't give any more, or know any more than at first.

A church that doesn't grow dies. A Christian that doesn't grow dries up and blows away.

3. No Teamwork

> Vs. 4-9 – For when one says, "I am of Paul," and another, "I am of Apollos," are you not mere men? What then is Apollos? And what is Paul? Servants through whom you believed, even as the Lord gave opportunity to each one. I planted, Apollos watered, but God was causing the growth. So then neither the one who plants nor the one who waters is anything, but God who causes the growth. Now he who plants and he who waters are one; but each will receive his own reward according to his own labor. For we are God's fellow workers; you are God's field, God's building.

Here Paul describes the ideal teamwork that goes on for the kingdom to grow. Each has a job, does a job, relies on each other to do the job, and gives God the glory for the final growth and results.

In Corinth they were jockeying for position, wanted glory, applause, power and control.

Someone once said, "You can accomplish anything if you don't care who gets the credit"; imagine what can be accomplished if everyone is anxious for God to get the credit!

4. Poor Teaching

> Vs. 10 – According to the grace of God which was given to me, like a wise master builder I laid a foundation, and another is building on it. But each man must be careful how he builds on it.

In this section Paul warns that poor teaching is like poor workmanship in a building; eventually the lack of quality will show.

Hosea said, "My people are destroyed for lack of knowledge" Hosea 4:6.

Good Bible teaching will build the church, and poor teaching, from cradle roll to the pulpit, will destroy it. Teaching is an important responsibility and we need to understand that everybody's class or group is very important in the overall building of the church.

5. Tampering with the Temple

> Vs. 16-17 – Do you not know that you are a temple of God and that the Spirit of God dwells in you? If any man destroys the temple of God, God will destroy him, for the temple of God is holy, and that is what you are.

These people were hard living types who abused their bodies with what they consumed (food and drink) as well as what they did (sex). The reason for this was that their Greek heritage taught them that what you did to your body didn't affect your soul (concept of Dualism).

Paul corrects this false notion by pointing out that the proper use of the body is to provide a dwelling place not only for the soul but also for the Holy Spirit of God. You can't grow as a Christian or a church if you constantly abuse and insult the Holy Spirit with bad treatment to His temple.

6. Over the Edge

> 4:6 – For I am conscious of nothing against myself, yet I am not by this acquitted; but the one who examines me is the Lord.

Today, being on the edge or going over the edge is fashionable and applauded. We admire people who take risks.

When it comes to God's word, however, safety is the operative word. The key is to do *exactly* what it says, no more or less. The smallest incorrect variation from God's word can take us far away from God's will and purpose, and sometimes over the edge into disobedience and disbelief.

7. Poor Role Models

> Vs. 14-16 – I do not write these things to shame you, but to admonish you as my beloved children. For if you were to have countless tutors in Christ, yet you would not have many fathers, for in Christ Jesus I became your father through the gospel. Therefore I exhort you, be imitators of me.

The Corinthian leaders were involved in a battle for prestige and power, and the disciples joined the fray. In the absence of good leadership models Paul offers himself as a pattern of Godliness, service and perseverance.

A group rarely rises above its leadership, and in the church this is true as well. Jesus is our Lord and ultimate leader, but human beings learn how to become like the Lord from those around them.

The church grows only in proportion to its leadership. If the leaders don't grow, neither will the church. One thing that kills church growth is the refusal of its leaders to grow. When the time for judgment arrives, they will be held accountable.

8. Immorality

> 5:1 – It is actually reported that there is immorality among you, and immorality of such a kind as does not exist even among the Gentiles, that someone has his father's wife.

There are many sins we struggle with each day but sexual sins are the most devastating. They hurt our own souls because they cause great shame and guilt. They hurt our families because they destroy relationships and friendships. They hurt the church because the effect of sexual sin often causes many to abandon Christ, both the guilty and those who are the victims.

Before you say yes to sexual temptation or sexual situations, ask yourself if the few minutes of pleasure will be worth all the broken lives, the tears and possibly your soul.

9. Ignorance

> 6:9-11 – Or do you not know that the unrighteous will not inherit the kingdom of God? Do not be deceived; neither fornicators, nor idolaters, nor adulterers, nor effeminate, nor homosexuals, nor thieves, nor the covetous, nor drunkards, nor revilers, nor swindlers, will inherit the kingdom of God. Such were some of you; but you were washed, but you were sanctified, but you were justified

> in the name of the Lord Jesus Christ and in the Spirit of our God.

Some people know the word and the love of God, but ignore the terrible judgment that God promises those who disobey Him. Sometimes in the church we are careless with our faith, service, attendance and giving because we ignore the fact that God will reject lukewarm Christians as violently as He will the ones mentioned in this verse. Fear is not the best motivation to serve God, but it is a valid one and one that God will accept.

A church that ignores the fact that it will be judged becomes lazy and careless.

10. Ingratitude

> Vs. 19-20 – Or do you not know that your body is a temple of the Holy Spirit who is in you, whom you have from God, and that you are not your own? For you have been bought with a price: therefore glorify God in your body.

Paul says in Romans 1:21 that man's primary sin is that he did not glorify and thank God for what he had.

These Corinthians were so busy taking credit that they were missing the point that their purpose for being together was to glorify God, not each other.

A growing church is one where worship, both public and private, is filled with a sense of appreciation and joy for being disciples of Jesus Christ.

Summary

I suppose this chapter has some interest if we are looking at why the Corinthian church wasn't growing, but it takes on a much greater importance if we apply it to ourselves.

We need to ask ourselves if some of the things Paul spoke to them about could be re-directed towards ourselves if He were addressing our congregation instead of the Corinthians.

4.
FLEE FORNICATION

I CORINTHIANS 6:18

Before we discuss the next topic from I Corinthians, I'd like to give a description of some popular TV shows being re-run on various channels. This is how TV Guide describes them:

- Friends – The characters of the popular "Friends" series imagine the various sexual combinations that they could have had in a "what if" dream sequence. Situations include threesomes and MORE.

- Veronica's Closet – A series from 2000 with Kirstie Alley being broadcast in repeats, describes one episode in the following way. Josh continually denies his homosexuality even though he constantly flirts with Kevin, the wedding coordinator for his wedding.

Josh's fiancée, also enamored with Kevin, faxes him a picture of herself in the nude.

I mention these because public sexual immorality is nothing new.

In Paul's letter to the Corinthians he deals with the same kinds of problems. The Gentile Christians in that church had a very different background when it came to sexual conduct than their Jewish brothers. Many of them were familiar with the practice of having sex with temple prostitutes, and Paul refers to a case of incest actually going on in the church (I Corinthians 5:1-3).

So, there were problems of sexual immorality in their society as well as the church of that time; and nothing has changed. I could go on to describe show after show, movie after movie, that all have one common denominator, regardless of their characters or storylines. Each one of them condones and promotes fornication as something normal and consequence free. You see, every program and situation I described to you before:

- Whether it included the free and friendly sex on "Friends."

- The homosexual and lesbian stories on other shows.

- The nudity, transgender characters and live-in sex repeated endlessly in movie after movie.

All these forms of sexual identity and activity come under the umbrella of one single word in the Bible: fornication.

Fornication is not truly an English word. The Greek word for illicit sex in the New Testament was porneia. This word was first translated into the Latin word fornicare, which meant brothel. When English translations appeared, the Latin word fornicare became the English word fornicate.

With time, the English word "fornicate" came to represent all forms of illicit or forbidden sexual practices including:

- Adultery – sex outside of marriage by a married person
- Homosexuality – sex between two men or two women
- Pedophilia – sex between an adult and a child
- Pornography – depiction of sex in print, film or live shows
- Beastiality – sex between humans and animals

In other words, fornication is sexual immorality, and sexual immorality is sexual activity outside the boundaries of marriage.

I've gone into detail about this word because there is such a permissive attitude today about fornication, even among Christians. Thankfully, believers still see the seriousness and sinfulness of various types of fornication like adultery, homosexuality and pedophilia, however, there seems to be a greater acceptance of sexual intimacy and sexual intercourse by men and women outside of marriage. It seems that Christians are as opposed as ever to unfaithfulness in marriage and various sexual perversions, but are more accommodating to heterosexual relations before people are married. There was a time when there was considerable shame and guilt if a couple fell into temptation and had sex before they were married. Today, it seems that the only time we feel ashamed or guilty of sin is if our pre-marital sexual activity produces a pregnancy or disease.

To remind us and caution us concerning these pervasive and powerful elements in our lives, I'd like to review some of the important teachings the Bible sets forth on the subject of fornication and a key admonishment about it in I Corinthians chapter 6.

Bible Teaching on Fornication

Fornication is Sinful

Whenever the Bible mentions fornication it is always in the context of sin. There is no such thing as moderate fornication, or good fornication; it is always bad.

Jesus Himself specifically mentions this activity as being sinful.

> For out of the heart come evil thoughts, murders, adulteries, fornications, thefts, false witness, slanders. These are the things which defile a man
> - Matthew 15:19-20a

Note the various activities He mentions along with fornication: murder, stealing, lying, etc.

No one, especially Christians, would doubt for a moment that these things are wrong; they are immoral, evil, against God and against man as well. And yet, we doubt at times the seriousness of the sexual sin of fornication. Make no mistake, fornication is a sin, it was a sin when Jesus taught about it to His Apostles and it remains a sin today.

<u>All</u> Fornication is Sinful

This point may seem redundant to you but there is a reason why I am reemphasizing it. Many Christians, especially younger ones, are beginning to make distinctions among the various sexual activities covered by the biblical term "fornication." They see as wrong and sinful those sexual practices that they feel are perverted and disgusting: child molestation, homosexuality, beastiality.

But, certain sexual activity that is promoted and accepted by this society and the media, this is ok:

- Sex between two people who may not be married but who love each other.

- Casual sex between friends that may not include intercourse but permit oral sex, nudity, various ways of stimulating and satisfying each other's sexual feelings.

In other words, there is this effort today to pick and choose within the different activities of fornication and make some acceptable. But the Bible does no such thing. When Jesus condemned fornication, He condemned the child molester and the couple having sex before marriage in the same sentence.

The only acceptable and blessed sexual union is that which God ordained between a man and a woman in marriage. All others are fornication, whether it be two lovers on a beach or the seller of pornography.

Fornication is Destructive

Some might be thinking, "Teaching #2 is pretty tough, who can accept it?" This is why there is Teaching #3 about the destructiveness of fornication.

The problem is that we can more readily see the destructive and dehumanizing affect that rape or molestation has on a person. This is why this form of fornication is easier to see as sin. But many, especially the young, don't always see the destructive nature of premarital sex between heterosexuals. This type of fornication is hard for them to see as sin. In the movies and on TV people are having sex all the time and they seem happy and satisfied.

The problem here is that TV and movies are make-believe. In the real world, pre-marital sex (whether it be full intercourse or partial sexual foreplay) has a negative, not positive, effect on people.

- Unplanned and unwanted pregnancies
- Sexually transmitted diseases
- Terrible feelings of guilt, shame, anger and resentment
- Feelings of loss
- For couples who have sex before marriage and go on to marriage, their marriage is twice as likely to have problems and divorce than the couple who waited until marriage to engage in sex – statistics, not doctrine!

And why these problems? Despite sex education, condom distribution, the glorification of sex in the media, the ridiculing of Christian views on sex – despite all of this, fornication, especially "the pre-marital sex" kind of fornication still causes problems. Why?

- Because God created sex and placed His boundaries on sex. Man didn't do this, God did.

- Because whenever man violates the boundaries that God has placed around sexual activities he will suffer, no matter what he thinks or says or does. "The wages of sin is death" (Romans 6:23).

- Because you cannot cross God's boundaries or laws without consequence, and that includes sexual boundaries.

So what are the boundaries?

- God has said that within marriage a man and a woman have a lifetime to enjoy, create, share and explore human sexuality to their hearts content (Genesis 2:23-24).

- This privilege and gift belongs exclusively to those who make a lifetime commitment to live as husband and wife.

- It is forbidden to all others and those who cross this boundary are guilty of the sin of fornication in one of its many forms.

God also says that there will be physical (which I mentioned before) and spiritual consequences for those who violate His command concerning fornication.

> Flee fornication. Every other sin that a man commits is outside the body, but the sexually immoral man sins against his own body.
> - I Corinthians 6:18

Here Paul summarizes the dangerous physical consequences that result from sexual sin.

> Or do you not know that the unrighteous shall not inherit the kingdom of God. Do not be deceived, neither fornicators, nor idolaters, nor adulterers, nor effeminate, nor homosexuals, nor thieves, nor the covetous, nor drunkards, nor revilers, nor swindlers, shall inherit the kingdom of God.
> - I Corinthians 6:9-10

This is pretty clear as to the sinfulness and seriousness of fornication. Paul teaches that those guilty of this sin will be lost, they will not go to heaven. We should take seriously an action that has the power to both ruin our physical and emotional health, as well as condemn our souls to hell.

Satan has seduced us into thinking that fornication is normal, healthy, even something better than purity, self-control and obedience. Let's not be fooled (or "deceived" as Paul says), fornication in all of its forms: Is an offense to God because it crosses the boundary which He has set for human sexuality, is destructive to one's body and emotion, and is the cause for losing one's soul.

People in the world write their own rules when it comes to sex. As Christians, however, we follow the rules written by God concerning this and other matters.

Flee Fornication

If I were to summarize all of what the Bible says about dealing with fornication in our lives, I could not do it better than what Paul says in I Corinthians 6:18, "Flee fornication."

In today's words: stay away, run away from every form of sexual sin. Every person has (for whatever reasons) weaknesses in the area of sexual feelings, desires and expression. Some are tempted to exhibitionism (they want to show themselves), for others it's pornography, for still others it may be the constant lure to be unfaithful; the most common is pre-marital sex.

Because of our sinful nature we are drawn to any number of forbidden sexual practices under the general heading of fornication. How do we, as Christians, deal with these temptations to sin sexually?

Remember Who We Are

We're not animals regulated solely by our feelings and our instincts. We are not unbelievers, slaves to sin and to whatever stimulus Satan puts in the world. We are Christians, washed in the blood of Christ, powered by the Spirit and instructed by God's word.

Our goal is not sexual gratification, our goal is higher and more satisfying than this: our goal is to please the God who saved us from sin and with whom we will live in purity forever.

> Therefore also we have as our ambition, whether at home or absent, to be pleasing to Him. For we must all appear before the judgment seat of Christ, that each one may be recompensed for his deeds in the body, according to what he has done, whether good or bad.
> - II Corinthians 5:9-10

Sex is for this life and this world. We are made for the world to come.

Remember Who We Belong To

The argument for much illicit sex is that this is my body and so long as it's consensual, I can have whatever sex I desire. This argument is false because it is based on a false premise: that our bodies belong to us. In reality, our bodies are given to us by God as a vessel to carry our eternal souls, also given to us by God. Just because non-believers reject this idea doesn't make it untrue.

A Christian understands that his life is a stewardship of the body given to him by God and redeemed by the blood of Christ. Our bodies belong to God twice over: once when He created us, and once again when He saved us through Jesus

Christ. Paul says that, "our body is not for fornication but for the Lord..." (I Corinthians 6:13)

Our bodies belong to God, and we must use our bodies to serve and honor Him. We can serve and honor God with our sexual activity but only when we keep it within the boundaries He has set, otherwise we dishonor ourselves and our Lord.

Remember To Flee

Since sexual power is so strong we need to remember that the best way to deal with temptation is to flee. Don't put yourself into situations with people or activities in such a way that you know you'll be tempted. Don't dress in such a way that invites sexual desire. Do decide and declare ahead of time what your boundaries are – to yourself and others.

We are weak sinners and easily fall, so take precautions and head for the hills at the first sign of temptation.

Remember Heaven

The hardest thing for people (especially young people) to do is to take a long view. But the issue of sexual sin is all about taking the short view over the long view. Sexual sin is short lived, a passing passion, usually over as quickly as it takes to lure us in. But the consequences are usually felt over a long period of time.

Remember the promise of heaven, remember the peacefulness and joy of a clear conscience, remember the strength that comes from doing what is right.

When not sure about the situation, ask yourself, "will this help me or hinder me from going to heaven?"

Summary

The ideas that you have just read about sex are rarely spoken in today's media concerning sex. This is because what you have heard today is what the Spirit says about sex. What you see in the world is what the flesh wants to hear about sex.

As Christians, young and old, remember what the Spirit says concerning the sin of fornication:

1. Fornication is a sin in all of its forms.

2. No matter how appealing and acceptable the world makes it look, fornication is always destructive.

3. Because of our weak flesh we need to make every effort to avoid people and situations that will lead us to sin in this way.

4. One last thing I'd like to remind you of is this: fornication, like every other sin can be forgiven. Paul says of those who were guilty of fornication, "And such were some of you, but you were washed, but

you were sanctified, but you were justified in the name of the Lord Jesus Christ, and in the Spirit of our God." (I Corinthians 6:11)

You see, sexual sins hurt us deeply, the scars are ugly and the damage is extensive. But, the Bible promises us that God's love and forgiveness go even deeper to heal the damage, repair the scars and stop the pain caused by sexual sin.

Those who confess Christ, repent of this and every other sin and are washed in the blood of Christ through baptism are given a purity that the past cannot erase or take away.

5.
KEEPING THE LOCK IN WEDLOCK

I CORINTHIANS 7:1-40

One of the most difficult issues in the church is the one concerning marriage and divorce. For this reason, I'd like to review some principles and teachings about marriage and divorce found throughout the Bible, up to and including Paul's teaching on the subject in I Corinthians 7.

There are many things that you may or may not agree with here and that's OK. I offer these points as a summary of my own studies over the years, studies that I am continually adding to.

The Base Model

It is interesting to note that marriage is the first social unit established by God. In Genesis 2:22-25 we see five elements of this union.

> The Lord God fashioned into a woman the rib which He had taken from the man, and brought her to the man. The man said, "This is now bone of my bones, and flesh of my flesh; she shall be called Woman, because she was taken out of Man." For this reason a man shall leave his father and his mother, and be joined to his wife; and they shall become one flesh. And the man and his wife were both naked and were not ashamed.

1. Man and woman are the same in nature, both created by God and expressly made for each other.

2. The marriage unit consists of only one man and one woman. This is the model blessed by God (not two men, two women or three women and one man, etc.)

3. The union of a man and his wife supersedes the union of these people with their parents. When men and women marry, their new relationship takes priority over their relationship with parents. The marriage bond does not eliminate the parental bond, it takes priority over it.

4. The marriage union is exclusive (one flesh) and cannot be entered into by any other individual, in any way. I believe that this includes artificial insemination by a third party for childless couples.

5. Within marriage, human sexuality can be expressed freely and completely without shame, guilt or embarrassment.

In this passage no exceptions, punishments or prohibitions were further added because there was no sin and thus no need. The marriage model in Genesis is stated in completely positive terms because man was still perfect and without sin.

The Mosaic Model

Once sin enters the world, mankind is weakened to the point where everything is affected, including marriage.

- Where mutual respect and honor were once assured, there is now violence and disrespect, even slavery.

- Where formerly there would be a natural development of new families from existing ones, there is jealousy and possessiveness.

- Where fidelity and sexual exclusiveness is the norm, impurity and adultery become widespread.

- Where lifelong relationships are assumed, broken marriages and abandonment take place.

As a response to this, God, through Moses, allows certain laws to be put into place in order to mitigate or keep at a minimum the damage in marriage caused by sinfulness.

In Deuteronomy 24:1-4, one such law permitted a husband to legally divorce his wife if is she was sexually unfaithful.

> When a man takes a wife and marries her, and it happens that she finds no favor in his eyes because he has found some indecency in her, and he writes her a certificate of divorce and puts it in her hand and sends her out from his house, and she leaves his house and goes and becomes another man's wife, and if the latter husband turns against her and writes her a certificate of divorce and puts it in her hand and sends her out of his house, or if the latter husband dies who took her to be his wife, then her former husband who sent her away is not allowed to take her again to be his wife, since she has been defiled; for that is an abomination before the Lord, and you shall not bring sin on the land which the Lord your God gives you as an inheritance.

In this passage Moses also protects the woman from being unjustly passed around from man to man by forbidding the original husband from re-marrying her. The law said you couldn't remarry your ex-wife! This establishes sexual sin as a valid reason to divorce, something not mentioned in Genesis because this sin did not exist then. Notice the development of teaching to address new problems and circumstances.

The Gospel Model

It's interesting to note that many people think Jesus added the exception of adultery or fornication to the teaching on marriage and divorce. People call it the "exception clause" in Matthew 19:9:

> ...whoever divorces his wife, except for immorality and marries another woman commits adultery.

Jesus added nothing new to what had already been written in the Law. He merely clarified the interpretation that some scribes were giving to Deuteronomy 24:1-4. Some were saying that you could divorce your wife for any reason, so long as you did the paperwork; and some said, no, the Law said you could only justify divorce when there was sexual immorality.

Jesus responded to the argument by reminding them that God still held them to the original model as their basis for marriage and that, according to the Law, only sexual immorality was a just cause for divorce.

There are many other issues regarding marriage but this is the only one that Jesus addressed during His ministry. Later on in the epistles, Paul will discuss other subjects.

The Apostolic Model

There are many things that the gospel writers did not record in the gospels that were later written about in the epistles:

- Indwelling of the Holy Spirit (Acts 2:38)

- Various Gifts (I Corinthians)

- Organization of the church (I Timothy)

Many new ideas that don't contradict or confuse established ones not found in the gospels are discussed in the letters of the Apostles and this is in accordance with what Jesus had told His Apostles would eventually happen.

> I have many more things to say to you, but you cannot bear them now. But when He, the Spirit of truth, comes, He will guide you into all the truth; for He will not speak on His own initiative, but whatever He hears, He will speak; and He will disclose to you what is to come. He will glorify Me, for He will take of Mine and will disclose it to you. All things that the Father has are Mine; therefore I said that He takes of Mine and will disclose it to you.
> - John 16:12-15

Jesus would continue to reveal His will and purpose to the Apostles concerning their work and the church through the Holy Spirit. I say this because in I Corinthians 7 there is information about marriage which is not contained in the gospels but helps us deal with the problems encountered by people in situations not addressed by Jesus, but very common.

This teaching Paul obviously received from the Holy Spirit in order to respond to the question that Christians had at that time (they needed information not found in the gospels). I'll summarize the main points Paul makes about marriage in chapter 7.

Celibacy and Marriage are Both Blessed by God

> Now concerning the things about which you wrote, it is good for a man not to touch a woman. But because of immoralities, each man is to have his own wife, and each woman is to have her own husband. The husband must fulfill his duty to his wife, and likewise also the wife does not have authority over her own body, but the husband does; and likewise also the husband not have authority over his own body, but the wife does. Stop depriving one another, except by agreement for a time, so that you may devote yourselves to prayer, and come together again so that Satan will not tempt you because of your lack of self-control. But this I say by way of concession, not of command. Yet I wish that all men were even as I myself am. However, each man has his own gift from God, one in this manner, and another in that.

> But I say to the unmarried and to widows that it is good for them if they remain even as I. But if they do not have self-control, let them marry; for it is better to marry than to burn with passion.
> - I Corinthians 7:1-9

It seems that some thought that being celibate was a higher calling than being married but were feeling bad because they couldn't manage it. There may even have been some who were married and were trying to abstain from sex in order to please the Lord.

Paul tells them that people, being who they are, need to be married, and when they are they should give themselves fully to one another in sexual union (only abstaining by mutual consent and only for a short time). Paul tells them that celibacy has its advantages but is only for those who have been given the ability to live this way by God. Marriage is God's gift to man in order to deal with and find satisfaction for normal human sexual desire without sinning.

Keep the Lock in Wedlock – 7:10-24

In the next section Paul addresses two groups concerning marriage break-ups.

> Vs. 10-11 – But to the married I give instructions, not I, but the Lord, that the wife should not leave her husband (but if she does leave, she must remain unmarried, or else be reconciled to her husband), and that the husband should not divorce his wife.

Christians married to each other should remain that way.

This was a necessary teaching because among Greeks and Romans there were many classifications of marriages. Slave marriages were considered non-binding (not legal) and couples could be split-up and sold separately. Marriages between slave and free were seen as loose associations and easily dissolved.

Paul is saying that as Christians, regardless of their position in life, if they were married it was binding before God. He also specifies that if they are separated they have two choices: to live like unmarried, meaning not to engage in any sexual union with someone else as what would be expected of a Christian single person; or return to the marriage.

These two options did not involve sin. This is what Paul is trying to explain here (what can we do in difficult situations and avoid sinning). This is completely in line with Jesus' teaching. Paul says that married Christians should not divorce for any reason they wish. He doesn't mention the exception of fornication but it is assumed that they know about Jesus' teaching on this. They want clarification about their situation.

Christians married to non-believers.

> Vs. 12-16 – But to the rest I say, not the Lord, that if any brother has a wife who is an unbeliever, and she consents to live with him, he must not divorce her. And a woman who has an unbelieving husband, and he consents to live with her, she must not send her husband away.
>
> For the unbelieving husband is sanctified through his wife, and the unbelieving wife is sanctified through her believing husband; for otherwise your children are unclean, but now they are holy. Yet if the unbelieving one leaves, let him leave; the brother or the sister is not under bondage in such cases, but God has called us to peace. For how do you know, O wife, whether you will save your husband? Or how do you know, O husband, whether you will save your wife?

If the non-believer is willing to live with the believer in peace despite their faith difference, then remain married. There may have been some who thought that as Christians they may have been obliged to cut off their relationships with non believing (pagan) spouses as did the Jews who divorced their foreign pagan wives at God's command in Ezra 10. But Paul sees this as a different case not subject to laws that governed who the Jews would and could not marry in the Old Testament. Jewish Christians may have had some sensitivity to this idea but not Gentiles to whom much of this teaching is directed. He even says that such unions are sanctified (blessed/legitimate) because of the presence of the Christian in the marriage.

If the non-believer leaves, let him/her go. It seems that by his answer some believed that if they remained loyal to the relationship, they might save their partner in some vicarious way. But Paul tells them that they have no control over this once they've been abandoned, so they should just let go and live in peace.

The word Paul uses "...not under bondage..." (verse 15) is a word that denotes slavery. The idea is that in the event of abandonment, the Christian is no longer enslaved, bound or tied to the other individual or the marriage. In this entire passage Paul has been talking about marriage and divorce so his meaning here in context and in word is very clear. If abandoned, the Christian is freed from that marriage without committing a sin.

Now just in case there are some who think this is a new teaching or new interpretation of I Corinthians 7, I want to remind you what Alexander Campbell (an early leader of the Restoration Movement and great biblical scholar) wrote, "..it seems to me that in all cases of voluntary desertion on the side of the unbelieving party, the marriage covenant is made void and the believing party is to the deserter as though they had never been married." (Millennial Harbinger V5, P72)

Other early Restorationists like Walter Scott and writers such as R.L. Whiteside also held to this view. Let us remember that the base model is always the one we work with, but through Moses, Jesus and Paul, God responds to and deals with the outcomes of marriages that have been attacked by sexual sins, human weaknesses and desertion. I acknowledge that there are different points of view on these issues but this is the conclusion I have come to on what Paul teaches in I Corinthians 7.

Lest we forget the original point: Paul points out three important things concerning the questions that the Corinthians are asking about marriage:

1. Both marriage and celibacy are blessed.

2. The base model is always to stay married, but if your unbelieving spouse leaves you, let him go, you are not bound.

3. Marriage is normal, but being single and dedicated to the Lord has many advantages.

In those times there was great persecution of Christians and so to marry meant the possible risk to home and family from attack. Paul prepares those who marry to be ready for the suffering they may have to endure. He also reminds those who are able to remain single that a life wholly dedicated to God has many joys and blessings:

1. Less worries about worldly things, no burden of family.

2. Greater freedom to serve and know the Lord.

3. Freedom to go and do things on behalf of the kingdom (i.e. missions).

It depends on the place God has put you, but the choice of either life (celibate or married) will have its challenges and blessings.

Summary

There are many questions surrounding marriage, divorce and re-marriage. Paul deals with some specific cases here that were troubling the Corinthian church at that time.

In the end, God calls on us to live faithfully with our partners until death. He gives instructions for when there are problems but this is always the ideal. There are times when divorce is justified, but remember that it is never without sin, pain, sorrow and guilt – even if you are the victim.

6.
SINGLE SOLUTIONS

I CORINTHIANS 7:25-35

I'd like to double back to chapter 7 of I Corinthians and pick up an idea that pertains to a specific group in the church: those who are single.

It seems to me that the life of the single/unmarried adult is plagued by the following problems:

- Waiting – For a new situation to develop whether it is a job, education or especially a relationship. When it comes to relationships it is always the painful waiting to see if this person is the "right" one, or the fear of being hurt.

- Worry – You worry about direction and making right decisions and yet have so little information with which to make them. It seems that everything is always "in the air" and that can be stressful.

- Loneliness – Christian single adults cannot experience satisfying sexual relationships without guilt and disappointment. It's hard to develop deep emotional bonds and receive comfort from a loving partner without sexual intimacy. In a world of couples, a single person seems to be perpetually on the outside looking in.

The problem facing the single person is that eventually much of his/her emotional energy becomes focused on simply waiting, worrying and feeling lonely. The result of this is that many singles:

- Become impatient and begin making foolish commitments to people and things that are wrong for them.

- They pay too much attention to their own problems and needs which only intensifies the feeling of depression.

- They go from being alone, to feeling lonely; quite a different thing.

This cycle of worry, loneliness and depression can make the single life more difficult than it needs to be. In chapter 7 of 1

Corinthians Paul talks to singles and provides them with some solutions to their particular problems.

Recognize your state for what it is – 7:25-28

> Vs. 25 – Now concerning virgins I have no command of the Lord, but I give an opinion as one who by the mercy of the Lord is trustworthy.

Jesus never talked about this directly so Paul, as an inspired Apostle, teaches on the subject. The word "virgins" refers to a single person who had never married. The term "unmarried" was used to refer to widows and those single because of divorce.

> Vs. 26 – I think then that this is good in view of the present distress, that it is good for a man to remain as he is.

Jews considered it a disgrace to be single, but Paul says that being single is not something to be despised. Jesus was single. Paul was "unmarried." The single state is different from being married, but not inferior in God's sight. In those times it was easier to remain single because Christians were persecuted and married Christians had more to lose, so it was wiser to "remain unmarried."

> Vs. 27-28 – Are you bound to a wife? Do not seek to be released. Are you released from a wife? Do not seek a wife. But if you marry, you have not sinned; and if a virgin marries, she has not sinned. Yet such will have trouble in this life, and I am trying to spare you.

He reminds them that they shouldn't try to change their state, but if they marry they are not sinning, they just need to be aware of the risks. Whether married or single, God blesses both states. This should help us when anxious or waiting. We need to be assured that being single is acceptable to God. He can bless us and provide us with joy whether single or married. Singles may be impatient, but God is not impatient with a person because they are single! Being married isn't better or easier, it's just different.

Recognize the world for what it is – vs. 29-31

> Vs. 29-31 – But this I say, brethren, the time has been shortened, so that from now on those who have wives should be as though they had none; and those who weep, as though they did not weep; and those who rejoice, as though they did not rejoice; and those who buy, as though they did not possess; and those who use the world, as though they did not make full use of it; for the form of this world is passing away.

Paul reminds them that this world is passing away. The term "form of this world" is a theatrical term used to describe the situation where one act is over and a new group of actors and scenes are about to come on stage. This is the state of the world.

The Apostle is saying that whether happy, sad, unmarried or married, we need to remember that this world is only temporary; we, as Christians, are only passing through; and singleness and marriage are only for this world, not the next.

This realization should produce two things:

1. It should lower our concern and emotional investment in situations and things that are only temporary. In order to get the proper perspective on things, ask yourself the question, "How important will this be to me in one hundred years from now?"

2. Recognizing the temporariness of the world should help us focus on the world that is to come. A world which is represented here and now by:

   - The Word of God

   - The church of Christ

   - The Holy Spirit

This is where our emotional and intellectual energy needs to be invested: in the world to come, not in this temporary place.

Recognize the differences between the priorities of the single life and the married life – vs. 32-35

A Christian has to live in the world but he/she lives for the Lord, whether single or married. The single person, however, has more time and resources to devote to this first priority. The married person's first commitment is also to the Lord but in marrying, that commitment is primarily carried out by serving one's family (what a lot of husbands and wives don't understand when they decide to marry). Paul is not degrading this service, he is merely reminding them that this is the choice we make when we marry (to serve spouse and children in the name of Christ).

The single person's advantage is that he/she does not carry this burden of responsibility, and so is free to offer the Lord a wider range of time, talents and services. In the church the reverse often happens. It is the married people who carry the bulk of the responsibility for service; they do the majority of teaching, giving, visiting and serving, often to the neglect of their own families. Singles sometimes think their freedom belongs to them when in reality it belongs to the Lord.

When singles begin to make the Lord their first priority, not only does it benefit the church, but it also breaks the cycle of loneliness and depression caused by too great a focus on self.

Summary

Single life doesn't have to be a burden. If we recognize that being single is blessed by God, we can begin living for now and not see single life as just a waiting room area for the unmarried.

If we recognize the difference between what is temporary and eternal we'll stop worrying about what is passing away and pay more attention to what is truly valuable: the word, the church and souls.

If we recognize that our first priority (single or married) is pure and sincere service to the Lord then two things will happen: the Lord will draw near to us and we will be drawn into other peoples' lives through Him. This will be the deathblow to our loneliness and depression.

Are you single?

Make the most of your life for what it is now and serve God with enthusiasm knowing that He knows about your state and blesses it.

Don't worry, God is the one who cares for you whether you are single or married, and He will see to your needs whatever they are.

Remember that marriage is neither a solution nor a promotion but rather an opportunity to give yourself to one person instead of sharing yourself with many.

7.
LICENSE TO LOVE

I CORINTHIANS 8:1-13

As Christians, we understand that the Bible is the guide we use to direct our lives. Even though we may not always want or are able to do what it says, we are usually able to use it as a way to judge if our actions are right or wrong.

Many times this is easy to figure out.

- Murder is wrong.
- Adultery is wrong.
- Lying and stealing are wrong.
- Loving others is right.
- Worshiping God is good, etc.

When giving reasons why someone "ought" to do or not do something, we can point to the Bible and say that it tells us in black and white what we should or should not be doing. Now, as I said, we may not agree or may not always do what it says but at least its instructions are, for the most part, clear.

Problems arise when the Bible requires us to use judgment or discretion in order to get our answers.

1. Judgment – This is when we make a decision based on the general principles found in the Bible because there are no specific instructions to guide us.

Birth Control. There are no specific instructions about birth control in the Bible. Each couple has to base its decision on broad principles such as not harming an existing life (Exodus 20:13); maintaining the health of the mother (Luke 10:27); parents seeking the wisdom to know if they are capable of raising an additional child (Proverbs 2:6), etc. Broad principles that help us make a judgment call.

2. Discretion – This is where we make a decision based not only on broad principles found in the Bible (because there are no specifics), but we also factor in the effect that our decision will have on other people, especially Christians.

The decisions based on discretion are usually the most difficult to make because they are different for each person, and require a great amount of self-sacrifice. They usually involve things that are not in themselves bad but may be interpreted as being evil, perhaps unchristian or unorthodox by others. The dilemma is usually expressed in this manner, "Why should I deny myself such and such just because it might offend someone else?"

Paul received this kind of question from the Corinthian church and in his reply tells them how to deal with issues that require the use of discretion.

In first century Greece there were many pagan temples devoted to various gods, and each had its own ceremonies, including animal sacrifices. Unlike the Jewish sacrificial system where the animal was destroyed and its remains were eaten by the priest and the ones offering the sacrifice; the meat used in pagan rituals was often sold to public markets after the ritual was complete. Eating the sacrificed animal by the worshipper and priests was not required as it was in Jewish worship.

The problem, then, was that there were some Christians who were buying meat at the markets where some of the animals had originally been used in pagan sacrifice. Certain Christians disapproved of this and were offended because they felt that their Christian brethren were, in some indirect way, involving themselves in pagan sacrifice. Their argument went something like this:

- If you buy this kind of meat, you are supporting and participating in the pagan sacrificial system.

Today the same argument is made using different elements:

- Some Christians won't shop at certain stores because the company pays benefits to partners of gay employees. They feel to shop there is to support gay rights.

In teaching them, Paul deals with two issues.

1. The specific issue:
Is eating this meat a sin?

This was the debate that the brethren were having in Corinth. Concerning this question of sin Paul says three things.

1. Only those who practice idolatry are guilty of idolatry. Christians recognize only God and His Son, Jesus Christ. For Christians, idols are nothing more than wood and stone, and meat used in whatever way is only meat for a Christian. Christians eat with the understanding that all food comes from God regardless of what men may do or think about it in between time.

2. Not everyone is used to this idea, especially Greek Christians who have been raised to see idolatry and its practices as an important part of life. For a former

idolater, meat sacrificed to an idol has been tainted, and his conscience cannot help but see it as an offense against the true God. Of course, one problem here could have been the different backgrounds between Jews and Greeks who were in the same congregation.

3. Paul repeats a principle that Jesus taught (Mark 7:19). He says that food does not have the power to make you pleasing or not pleasing to God. God doesn't love vegetarians more than meat eaters. The Pharisees taught that if a Gentile touched certain foods that a Jew later purchased and ate, the Jew would become impure and need to purify himself before going to worship. Jesus taught that food by itself did not have the ability to purify or make you impure.

Paul repeats this idea here, stating that you couldn't "catch" immorality or idolatry from food as one catches a disease. Food was neutral, meat was just meat. So in response to the specific issue of sinfulness Paul says that:

*   The sin belongs to the idolaters and can't be transferred to the Christians through the meat.

*   Idolaters sin because they serve idols. Christians are righteous because they serve Christ, regardless of what they eat.

Now Paul moves from the specific issue to a broad principle, which is contributing to the problem.

2. The broad principle:
What to do when something isn't a sin
but your conscience feels like it is?

Sometimes we feel guilty and rightly so because according to the Bible we are doing something that we should not or we have neglected to do that we should. Sometimes, however, we feel guilty even though the Bible doesn't condemn our actions, only our conscience does.

This was the problem here; Paul has told them that there is no sin in eating this meat, but there are still some with guilty consciences. Again, his teaching is spread out through the chapter. He gives them three things to ponder:

1. Love is higher than knowledge

> 8:1-3 – Now concerning things sacrificed to idols, we know that we all have knowledge. Knowledge makes arrogant, but love edifies. If anyone supposes that he knows anything, he has not yet known as he ought to know; but if anyone loves God, he is known by Him.

He has given them knowledge about the legality of what they are doing; technically they are not wrong if they eat. But the guiding principle for our knowledge, he says, is love; and God knows the ones who love Him because it is evident in their actions. Those who love God use love in their application of knowledge. That we have knowledge is not what pleases God, it is how we use knowledge (in love) that pleases God.

2. License to love

> Vs. 9-12 – But take care that this liberty of yours does not somehow become a stumbling block to the weak. For if someone sees you, who have knowledge, dining in an idol's temple, will not his conscience, if he is weak, be strengthened to eat things sacrificed to idols? For through your knowledge he who is weak is ruined, the brother for whose sake Christ died. And so, by sinning against the brethren and wounding their conscience when it is weak, you sin against Christ.

You have knowledge and this knowledge has given you liberty (freedom in this case to eat) but be careful that you don't use your freedom selfishly.

God gives us liberty, freedom, license, but our license is not to indulge ourselves; our license is to be used for loving others.

In this instance, Paul describes a hypothetical situation: What if you use this freedom to indulge in this food, and a brother with a weak conscience copies your action (if he can, I can) but in doing so realizes that his conscience will not permit it and he feels guilty anyways? Paul doesn't say it, but the danger is that he may fall away or continue to do a lawful thing, but because he has a guilty conscience, for him a lawful thing becomes a sin.

In addition to this, Paul says that when they disregard the weak condition of this brother's situation and provide him with an excuse to violate his own conscience and thus sin, they are also guilty of sin!

Those who love God are free to live in Christ as they choose, but this freedom doesn't allow them to be free from the responsibility of caring for other people and their souls.

3. How far do we go?

> Vs. 13 – Therefore, if food causes my brother to stumble, I will never eat meat again, so that I will not cause my brother to stumble.

The fear here is that people will take advantage if we give up what we are allowed to do every time someone objects under the heading of being "offended." In other words: what good is freedom if we are prisoners of other peoples' weaknesses? In Romans 14:3-4 Paul gives further instructions to help avoid this kind of situation:

> The one who eats is not to regard with contempt the one who does not eat, and the one who does not eat is not to judge the one who eats, for God has accepted him. Who

> are you to judge the servant of another? To his own master he stands or falls; and he will stand, for the Lord is able to make him stand.
> - Romans 14:3-4

Basically he is speaking to both groups. Those who are strong (exercising their Christian liberty in good conscience and doing things that are not wrong) shouldn't be impatient, unloving or unkind to those who are weak in conscience and are not able to permit themselves the same things. There is to be no name-calling or accusations of legalism, narrow-mindedness, immaturity, etc. And those who he refers to as the "weak" should not act like judges over the actions of other Christians, especially when their criticism cannot be soundly supported by God's word.

Many times, it's not a question of truly being offended or stumbling. Paul says that to make someone stumble or to offend them means to influence them to do something that their own conscience will not permit.

Sometimes the "strong" use Christian freedom as an excuse to act or indulge in worldly activity (like gambling) or vices (smoking) without feeling guilty; and many times the "weak" say they are offended when in reality they are simply uncomfortable or jealous because someone is doing something they will not permit themselves to do. They then twist the scriptures or use the idea of church "tradition" as a means to deny others their rightful freedom in Christ.

When we criticize another for their actions and claim that we've been offended it better be because:

- A true sin according to the Bible has been committed.

- We have been provoked to violate our own conscience by the influence of another's actions.

If not, then we're merely judging our brothers and sisters according to our own standards, not God's standards. Both the weak and strong should leave the judging to God because it is God who will save both the strong and the weak according to His grace – not according to one's relative strength or weakness.

In the end, we have to go as far as we need to in order to guarantee that our actions do not contribute to the destruction of another's soul. That may not always be fair, but it will always be right. And in the end we want to do what is right, not just what is permitted or what is fair.

Summary

Not everything in Christianity is black or white. Sometimes we have to make decisions using:

- Judgment – assessing what we know about the word and making the best decision we can, given the circumstances.

- Discretion – not only using what we know about the Bible but also measuring the impact of our decision on the faith of someone else.

Paul teaches that we must not only consider what is lawful in order to please God, we must decide what is loving as well.

When God chose to save us He didn't do it based on:

- Law – According to law we should have been condemned and left to suffer in hell.

- Fairness – It wasn't fair that Jesus who did no sin, who always obeyed, should suffer our punishment for sin.

He based His decision on love, what was necessary in order to guarantee the salvation of our souls. That is the basis upon which our decisions should be made.

We need to ask God to forgive us and help us to mature spiritually if:

- We've violated our own conscience.

- We've encouraged, by our actions, someone else to violate theirs.

- We've accused others of sin for actions that are not really sin but just things that we don't like.

- We've been impatient with brethren who don't enjoy the same level of freedom in Christ that we do.

8.
FREEDOM THROUGH SLAVERY

I CORINTHIANS 9-10:33

One of the most precious blessings connected with living in this nation is the personal freedom we enjoy. We pride ourselves on this aspect of our lives, and measure our success and worth by the degree of freedom we have. The desire for greater personal freedom (to do what we want to do) drives the engine of our careers, and is the life long objective of many.

It is interesting to compare this approach and view of freedom with what Paul says about freedom in I Corinthians 9-10. Paul pursued freedom, but his approach was freedom through slavery. It seems odd that one could achieve freedom through such a thing as slavery, but that is exactly what Paul proposes to the Corinthians in this letter.

Of course, you have to understand that in first century Greece it was quite an advantage to be a "free" person in a society largely inhabited by slaves. Many of the Corinthian Christians were exactly in that situation; they were legally free men and women living in a city where slavery was common. This condition, it seems, had led them to feel proud and forget that freedom brought with it certain responsibilities.

In his letter, Paul reminds them of four areas where he has given up his freedom in order to guarantee the salvation of others, an example that he hopes will temper their pride.

1. Freedom to be compensated for his preaching

9:1-13 – Am I not free? Am I not an apostle? Have I not seen Jesus our Lord? Are you not my work in the Lord? If to others I am not an apostle, at least I am to you; for you are the seal of my apostleship in the Lord.

My defense to those who examine me is this: Do we not have a right to eat and drink? Do we not have a right to take along a believing wife, even as the rest of the apostles and the brothers of the Lord and Cephas? Or do only Barnabas and I not have a right to refrain from working? Who at any time serves as a soldier at his own expense? Who plants a vineyard and does not eat the fruit of it? Or who tends a flock and does not use the milk of the flock?

I am not speaking these things according to human judgment, am I? Or does not the Law also say these things? For it is written in the Law of Moses, "you shall not muzzle the ox while he is threshing." God is not concerned about oxen, is He? Or is He speaking altogether for our sake? Yes, for our sake it was written, because the plowman ought to plow in hope, and the thresher to thresh in hope of sharing the crops. If we sowed spiritual things in you, is it too much if we reap material things from you? If others share the right over you, do we not more? Nevertheless, we did not use this right, but we endure all things so that we will cause no hindrance to the gospel of Christ. Do you not know that those who perform sacred services eat the food of the temple, and those who attend regularly to the alter have their share from the alter?

Paul claims that he is a legitimate Apostle because he has seen the Lord and established them in Christ through his preaching. He points to the other Apostles and reminds them that they travel with their wives. It seems that he also includes the earthly brothers of the Lord in this group. He also refers to the scriptures that teach that the one who works at something deserves to profit or be paid by that enterprise.

After establishing his right to receive payment for his work according to the example of the other Apostles, according to the teaching of scripture and according to the history of the Jewish priesthood, he declares that he has given up that right in order to maintain a higher principle.

> Vs. 14 – So also the Lord directed those who proclaim the gospel to get their living from the gospel.

He summarizes the freedom and right he has been given by the Lord Himself to be paid for preaching.

> Vs. 15 – But I have used none of these things. And I am not writing these things so that it will be done so in my case; for it would be better for me to die than have any man make my boast an empty one.

He says this not to get them to pay him what he has a right to; he'd rather die than have someone accuse him of preaching for money.

> Vs. 16-18 – For if I preach the gospel, I have nothing to boast of, for I am under compulsion; for woe is me if I do not preach the gospel. For if I do this voluntarily, I have a reward; but if against my will, I have a stewardship entrusted to me. What then is my reward? That, when I preach the gospel, I may offer the gospel without charge, so as not to make full use of my right in the gospel.

He preaches for free in order to do two things:

1. To demonstrate that his preaching is a responsibility given to him by God. A thing he does whether he gets money or not because God has directed him to do it.

2. By giving up his right to be paid he can freely offer the gospel to everyone, not just those who can afford it.

Paul is free to receive payment but he gives up this freedom in order to gain the freedom to preach to everyone who will listen, without reference to money.

2. Freedom from tradition and opinion

> Vs. 19-23 – For though I am free from all men, I have made myself a slave to all, so that I may win more. To the Jews I became as a Jew, so that I might win Jews; to those who are under the Law, as under the Law though not being myself under the Law, so that I might win those who are under the Law; to those who are without law, as without law, though not being without the law of God but under the law of Christ, so that I might win those who are without law. To the weak I became weak, that I might win the weak; I have become all things to all men, so that I may by all means save some. I do all things for the sake of the gospel, so that I may become a fellow partaker of it.

As a Christian, Paul had only one Lord. He was free from religion, culture, tradition and other people's opinions. As a Christian his only Lord was Jesus, His only Law, the word of Christ. As he travelled and preached to various groups, however, he gave up this freedom and subjected himself to:

- Religion – he preached in synagogues (Acts 13), he preached in Greek schools (Acts 17).

- Tradition – he took vows to placate the Jews and went to the temple (Acts 21).

- Culture – he took Timothy along, a Greek, and circumcised him to avoid controversy (Acts 16).

He didn't have to do these things, they were all concessions to other peoples' beliefs, traditions, particular weaknesses – not his own. He did these things so that he might have access to different groups, and preach the gospel to those, who because of cultural, religious or personal barriers, would not hear the message of Jesus otherwise.

We don't always feel comfortable with other people's views or religious traditions but, like Paul, it is sometimes necessary to set aside our discomfort and judgment in order to have an opportunity to share our faith with them.

3. Freedom from the demands of the law

In this long passage from chapter 9:24-10:22, Paul explains that he is free from the demands of the Law and is now under grace.

- This means that he is now saved by a system of grace rather than by a system of Law.

- A person can be saved by the Law if that person obeys the Law perfectly: perfect obedience = salvation and eternal life.

Jesus was raised from the dead because He managed to be righteous according to the Law. He accomplished perfect obedience.

> Who committed no sin, nor was any deceit found in His mouth.
> - I Peter 2:22

Our problem is that we are not able to obtain salvation in this way, even if we understand the principle, we are not able to accomplish it. We always sin (Romans 3:23).

God devised a plan to save us despite our weakness. He sent Jesus to obtain salvation according to Law on our behalf by living a perfect life, offering that perfect life on the cross and then resurrecting to prove that God had accepted His life in exchange for ours. God then offered us salvation based on faith in Jesus rather than salvation based on perfect obedience; this is the system of grace or favor that the Bible talks about...this is the "good news."

So Paul says that he is saved by this system of grace. He doesn't have to be perfect in order to be saved anymore. In other words, he is free from the Law.

Now, you might think that a person who didn't have to be perfect would let things slide, but Paul says quite the opposite.

> 9:27 – But I discipline my body and make it my salve, so that, after I have preached to others, I myself will not be disqualified.

What he has been given for free is so precious that he is diligent in preserving it less he would, through carelessness, lose it.

In chapter 10 he uses the Israelites as an example of those who received great blessings and opportunities, but grew careless and consequently lost their way. In the case of the Corinthians he warns them to be careful that their freedom not lull them into complacency with the world.

Paul is free from the perfect demands of the Law because of grace, but he becomes a slave to personal holiness, self-control and purity so that sin will not take root in his life again and spoil his salvation or the salvation of others.

4. Freedom to do what his conscience permits

This idea is summarized in verses 23-24; 32-33.

> Vs. 23-24 – All things are lawful, but not all things are profitable. All things are lawful, but not all things edify. Let no one seek his own good, but that of his neighbor.
>
> Vs. 32-33 – Give no offense either to Jews or to Greeks or to the church of God; just as I also please all men in all things, not seeking my own profit but the profit of the many, so that they may be saved.

Paul was intelligent, well-travelled, well-educated and mature in the faith. He knew right from wrong and could discern the "grey areas." If he permitted himself something, he did it with a clear conscience. But in this passage he says that he is free to do what his conscience permits, but not at the expense of someone else's conscience.

And so, the boundary that Paul sets for his conduct had four sides:

1. That it did not offend or go against God and His word.

2. That it did not go against his own conscience.

3. That it did not go against the conscience of unbelievers.

4. That it did not offend the church.

He was free to say and do many things because of his superior knowledge and experience, but he restricted himself according to the knowledge and experience of others. Their conscience and limit became his limit. This was not fair, this was not easy, but this was definitely Christlike.

> Who although He existed in the form of God did not regard equality with God a thing to be grasped, but emptied Himself, taking the form of a bondservant.
> - Philippians 2:6

Paul was free to say and do as he pleased but he gave up that freedom so he could say and do as God pleased for the sake of others.

Summary

Paul says that he has basically given up four freedoms:

1. Freedom to be paid for his work.

2. Freedom from tradition and opinions.

3. Freedom from the demands of the Law.

4. Freedom to follow his conscience.

Each of these are precious personal freedoms that he has willingly given up, but he has done so for two reasons:

1. So he can have the opportunity to preach the gospel to as many people as possible.

2. So that nothing he says or does becomes the reason why someone else loses their soul.

Paul became a slave of other peoples' customs, weaknesses and cultures so that he could freely offer the gospel to all and be free from any blame for someone losing their salvation.

This material gives us insight into Paul's motives and methods of working with people, but what are the lessons for us today?

Everybody's soul is important, not just our own.

We tend to circle the wagons when we are safe, but this is not God's way. God wants every soul to hear the gospel, and the thing most important next to our own soul's salvation should be the salvation of other souls. Remember that when you have a chance to confess Christ, when asked to invite people to church, when a special collection for mission work is taken souls are #1 in importance with God.

The boundary of our freedom is love.

We need to remember that the guiding principle in our dealings with other people, whether they are Christians or not, is love, not freedom. It is not about what I am free to do or not do, it is about what love would do in this situation. In Christ we are always free to love, and many times the greater the restriction placed upon us, the greater the love required from us.

9.
VEILS: CUSTOM OR COMMAND?

I CORINTHIANS 11:1-16

In the eleventh chapter of the Corinthian letter Paul will address the subject of the use of veils in that church. The issue for the Corinthians was not simply the idea of proper dress code; the true issue was the importance of what the wearing of the veil represented in their society, and what message they were giving by their use of these veils.

There are some places where the use of veils is still an issue today (Caribbean churches), but for most of us this chapter helps us learn about the proper way to discern between customs and commands.

Background

In those times there were a variety of customs regarding head coverings – Jewish women did, Jewish men didn't; Roman men did in their pagan worship, Greek men did not. Varying customs were brought into the church and the question of what was proper became an issue of contention.

In the following verses Paul responds to questions about this issue by stating that the solution to their disagreement is found in Christian "orderliness." His argument is that Christian worship is orderly and should be guided by the natural order already inherent in the creation. The problem was not the wearing or not wearing of veils, but their view of what was orderly.

Divine Order

> Vs. 1 – Be imitators of me, just as I also am of Christ.

This verse belongs to chapter 10 as a summary statement of what he has said about freedom and the responsibility of freedom; that the brethren should follow his lead in this.

> Vs. 2-3 – Now I praise you because you remember me in everything and hold firmly to the traditions, just as I delivered them to you. But I want you to understand that Christ is the head of every man, and the man is the head of a woman, and God is the head of Christ.

He begins to deal with the subject of veils. He praises them for their perseverance in his teaching and examples. A compliment to establish a point where he will add more teaching with the hope they will respond in similar fashion.

This teaching has to do with relationships.

- A woman is in subjection to her husband, his leadership is modified because of his own subordination to Christ, and even Jesus voluntarily submitted His life to God.

- The point is that there is an order divinely established between woman, man, Christ and God. This divine model is the pattern which he will use to solve the disorder in the church created by the issue of veils.

> Vs. 4 – Every man who has something on his head while praying or prophesying disgraces his head.

The veil was a sign of submission to another person in the thinking of that culture. A Christian man therefore, was not to pray with his head covered because it would disgrace or dishonor his "head," Jesus Christ. The reason for this was that only Christ was head over man in worship, no other man or institution. His uncovered head signified this fact.

> Vs. 5-6 – But every woman who has her head uncovered while praying or prophesying disgraces her head, for she is one and the same as the woman whose head is shaved. For if a woman does not cover her head, let her also have her hair cut off; but if it is disgraceful for a woman to have her hair cut off or her head shaved, let her cover her head.

A Christian woman, however, who prayed with her head uncovered dishonors her head which is her husband. In Paul's day it meant she repudiated his leadership. To do this was shocking in those days (being unveiled in public), and Paul compares it to being completely shaved, which was a sign of prostitution or unchastity.

Now, at this point we enter into the discussion about whether or not women should lead prayer in worship, but let's leave that aside for a minute and review what Paul is saying to these first century people about the use of veils:

1. There exists a natural order, divinely appointed in creation.

2. What we do in our worship of God ought to reflect that natural order to be considered decent and proper.

3. In practical terms then, men should pray without head-covering to reflect their leadership, Jesus Christ; women ought to pray with their heads covered in order to reflect their leadership, their husbands (or fathers for single women).

Prayer / Prophecy

With regards to women praying and prophesying, note that he doesn't say leading in prayer or teaching; simply praying and prophesying in general terms. The instructions for public worship will only begin later in the chapter.

At this point, Paul is talking about those times when it is proper for women to prophesy and pray. Women are not restricted from prophesying and prayer – only doing so in public assembly. I Corinthians 14:34-36 clarifies that this would not be in public assemblies so Paul is talking about other occasions where women were to pray and prophesy – they were to wear the head-covering.

In the mixed, public assembly, their silence was their sign of submission while the men prayed and prophesied.

At home, or women's gatherings or other instances where they could prophesy or pray, they wore the head-covering to signify their submission and respect.

The point, however, was not about veils, it was about how one did things in order to convey an attitude of respect and submission to God. These were not men's inventions but rather instructions from God.

Divine Reasoning

Now that he has explained what they should do and why, he goes on to give the Divine reasoning behind this teaching.

> Vs. 7-10 – For a man ought not to have his head covered, since he is the image and glory of God; but the woman is the glory of man. For man does not originate from woman, but woman from man; for indeed man was not created for the woman's sake, but woman for the man's sake. Therefore the woman ought to have a symbol of authority on her head, because of the angels.

Man's glory is that he is created first and to pray uncovered is to reflect that glory.

Both men and women are created equally in the image of God, but man's glory is that he was created first, not better. Woman's glory is that the human race continues through her. To recognize their glory is to recognize God and what God has done, not what man has done. Man did not create himself nor did he have any say in the order of creation.

Women praying uncovered are suggesting that they should be in man's place. This is shameful because it repudiates God's order and in that culture, the husband's position.

A woman should recognize her place in creation and reflect her belief and acceptance of this; the veil was that symbol at that time. The key is that Paul recognized that it was a cultural symbol of his day.

To shock society and shame her husband by refusing the veil would also offend angels who are themselves respectful of God's order and witnesses of men's affairs.

> Vs. 11-12 – However, in the Lord, neither is woman independent of man, nor is man independent of woman. For as the woman originates from the man, so also the man has his birth through the woman; and all things originate from God.

He reminds them that man's authority does not mean independence. We are united biologically and submitted to one another spiritually. This order is not meant to create dominance or competition (sin is what does that). This order is meant to create mutual dependence and glory to God in reflecting the divine order.

> Vs. 13-15 – Judge for yourselves: is it proper for a woman to pray to God with her head uncovered? Does not even nature itself teach you that if a man has long hair, it is a dishonor to him, but if a woman has long hair, it is a glory to her? For her hair is given to her for a covering.

Here Paul uses an example from nature to underscore his point. Some things are suggested by nature; for example, long hair on a man is un-natural but considered proper and beautiful on a woman.

- Natural because a woman's hair will grow longer than a man's in normal circumstances.

- Social custom supports and promotes this natural phenomena.

- Long hair on men has always been out of the ordinary (even Jews who did it, did it because of a vow, not because of style).

The point there is this: any social custom, such as the veil, which accentuates an idea suggested by nature, must be proper. In other words, social customs are ok if they reflect accurately what is natural and already in the Divine order.

> Vs. 16 – But if one is inclined to be contentious, we have no other practice, nor have the churches of God.

All the churches at that time were following this custom and the reasoning behind it.

Modern Applications

Paul says that they must respect customs that reflect Divine truth and order. The problem for us today is what to do when customs change, especially when we're caught in the middle of that change.

Some churches, even today, have female members wear head coverings because they feel that the instructions in this passage are binding for all time. Most do not because they believe that the teaching here is about custom not command.

Here are a few ideas on this passage that will help us when we have to discern between custom (cultural) and command (divine).

1. Customs change, commands never change

In the case of the Corinthians it was custom to wear the veil in order to show submission and respect. This was not invented by Apostles or commanded by God, it was already a custom that existed in many societies.

This custom was not in itself an eternal truth, it merely reflected an eternal truth in regards to the relationship of men and women before God. Since the custom accurately reflected the Divine truth, Paul commanded them not to change or rebel against the custom for fear of creating a bad witness.

With time, this custom changed as societies changed, and it no longer reflects eternal truth in our culture (i.e. the holy kiss was a custom then that reflected fellowship and unity; today, a hug and handshake. Foot washing – at that time a sign of welcome/submissive service; today, offering refreshments and a comfortable seat).

The command remains (to submit, to maintain the order of God, Christ, man, woman) but the customs that reflect this truth change.

We need to focus on ways to make sure we are keeping the command and not perpetuating meaningless customs, and that we don't violate the commands with customs that reflect disobedience.

2. Customs change slowly

I think the problem in Corinth was that those Christian women knew that they didn't need the veil to be submissive – this was a question of the heart and attitude (and still is). They wanted to run too far ahead of custom and in so doing created offenses.

We have the same problem today. A hundred years ago a woman who wore pants was on the edge, and if she wore pants to church then she was offensive. Today, customs have changed and we don't see either of these things as daring or offensive.

These customs changed slowly and I believe that it is not the role of Christians to be on the leading edge of these changes, but rather to adapt to them when they cause neither sensation nor offense. Of course, we should be leaders when it comes to doing what is right, opposing injustice etc., but when it comes to custom, I believe Paul teaches that we should go at the pace that does not cause offense.

This requires some in the church to have patience with the slow pace of change at times, and others to be tolerant when things don't remain as they were 50 years ago. Remember, we want to preserve commands not custom.

Summary

So Paul encourages the Corinthians to submit to those customs that reflect God's eternal truth as a way of honoring God and maintaining order in the church.

We do well to do the same while exercising patience and love toward one another as we experience the changes that are inevitable in every generation. We don't want to be ahead of the changes, but at the same time don't want to cling to meaningless customs and attitudes that only hinder the growth of the body.

10.
UNWORTHY COMMUNION

I CORINTHIANS 11:17-34

> 11:27 – Therefore whoever eats the bread or drinks the cup of the Lord in an unworthy manner, shall be guilty of the body and the blood of the Lord.

Has it ever dawned on you that there may be times when we take communion in a way that is displeasing to God; in a way that causes us to be guilty of sin rather than washed clean of sin?

In I Corinthians 11, Paul rebukes a situation in the Corinthian church that was causing them to partake in an unworthy manner.

Unworthy Communion in Corinth

As we will read in a moment, Paul has received news about the conduct going on at this church. Among other things: there was competition for leadership, sexual immorality, and disorder between men and women in regards to teaching and position.

In this passage we get a glimpse of what problems they were having in the area of public worship, especially in celebrating the Lord's Supper.

> Vs. 17 – But in giving this instruction, I do not praise you, because you come together not for the better but for the worse.

This verse is a bridge from the last set of instructions about veils and maintaining proper order between men and women. He says here that they have created disorder not only with the veil issue but with the next issue concerning the Lord's Supper as well.

> Vs. 18 – For, in the first place, when you come together as a church, I hear that division exist among you; and in part I believe it.

It is interesting to note that Paul makes a distinction here about "coming together as a church."

Individual members are Christians and members of the church wherever they are but there is a special entity that is created when individual Christians consciously come together as "a church." Three brothers getting together for coffee and fellowship are all members of the church but they do not constitute "a church" when they get together. 10,000 people converge at a Christian college to hear speakers and share fellowship. They belong to the body but they are not a congregation. Christians can be together without being "a church."

What transforms a fellowship of Christians into a gathering of "a church" are the rules that guide their purpose and conduct during their meeting.

Christians are always supposed to act in a holy and proper way but when they gather as "a church" there are some procedures, goals and activities that they are required to have and do that are not required when they meet in a casual way.

- There are no elders that oversee and direct a college lectureship, but if the same group decides to be "a church" they must select elders who will guide and oversee the group.

- No communion is served at a lectureship, but if the group were "a church" they would need to prepare and serve the Lord's Supper on Sundays.

- Lectureship has no duty to preach the gospel, care for the sick, etc., but if this group were to meet as "a church" they would be duty bound to carry out these tasks.

So if these brothers who are members of the church get together for coffee, all they have to do is have coffee. If they want to pray and encourage each other that is fine, and the Lord is among them, but they are not "a church." If these three brothers decide they want to be "a church" then they are required to function under the guidelines given by Jesus and the Apostles.

Paul is addressing this issue with the Corinthians. When they come together as "a church" they are bringing in many practices that are improper even outside the context of church life, let alone dragging them into the activity of the church.

> Vs. 18-21 – For, in the first place, when you come together as a church, I hear that divisions exist among you; and in part I believe it. For there must also be factions among you, so that those who are approved may become evident among you. Therefore when you meet together, it is not to eat the Lord's Supper, for in your eating each one takes his own supper first, and one is hungry and another is drunk.

He mentions four things that are improper not just in the church but outside the church as well.

1. Division – There are cliques and groups that are not in fellowship or exclusive to one another.

2. Competition – Different groups are supporting different leaders who are jockeying for position, like politics.

3. Unkindness – What was supposed to be a love feast (fellowship meal) becomes an occasion of offense. They usually had their gathering in the evening because many were slaves and had duties seven days a week. They would have an evening meal as part of their fellowship, and called this a "love feast." The wealthy who had food came early and ate, the slaves who had no food, who had to work until sundown, arrived hungry and too late to eat.

4. Revelry – Again, what is supposed to be a love feast turns into a pagan feast of excess where people get drunk. In New Testament times, Christians often shared a meal and had communion as a part of that meal. This was probably due to the fact that communion was instituted by Jesus during the Passover meal.

Vs. 22 – What! Do you not have houses in which to eat and drink? Or do you despise the church of God and

> shame those who have nothing? What shall I say to you? Shall I praise you? In this I will not praise you.

This verse is used by many to say that we are not allowed to eat in the building, and I respect those who feel this way and would not pressure them to go against their conscience, however, in those times the Apostles commented and participated in these love feasts (Paul did at Troas, Acts 20:7). Their teaching was that there should be true love and proper conduct during these times, not that the agape meals (what they were called) should be abolished.

In verse 22 Paul rebukes those who have been unkind. He doesn't say that you cannot have a love feast/agape meal (today: fellowship meal) rather, he instructs those who can't share or who can't wait for the participation of all to eat at home.

> Vs. 23-26 – For I received from the Lord that which I also delivered to you, that the Lord Jesus in the night in which He was betrayed took bread; and when He had given thanks, He broke it and said, "This is My body, which is for you; do this in remembrance of Me." In the same way He took the cup also after supper, saying "This cup is the new covenant in My blood; do this, as often as you drink it, in remembrance of Me." For as often as you eat this bread and drink the cup, you proclaim the Lord's death until He comes.

In these verses he reviews with them the purpose for the meeting and the meal in the first place: Jesus Christ. It's not about food or drink; it's not about who's first or who receives honor. The purpose for the church to gather is to honor Jesus Christ by sharing the Lord's Supper. The love feast is supposed to reflect the unity, love and nourishment of the entire body. What they were doing was the exact opposite.

Paul tells them that when they gathered together as "a church" it was for the express purpose of making a public statement that they were disciples of Jesus Christ. Communion was a silent witness of who they were and what they expected to happen. They were spoiling their witness by their conduct during the love feast. Paul tells them that if they can't do it correctly, they should stay at home to eat.

Paul now warns them about the possibility of taking communion in an unworthy manner, and the consequences of this.

> Vs. 27 – Therefore whoever eats the bread or drinks the cup of the Lord in an unworthy manner, shall be guilty of the body and the blood of the Lord.

A person who takes communion normally does so to signify that the body and blood of Christ removes their sins. To take communion improperly, as they were, has the opposite effect: it adds another sin to their charge. This is such a serious sin that Paul compares it to actually being guilty of crucifying the Lord all over again by their actions.

> Vs. 28-29 – But a man must examine himself, and in so doing he is to eat of the bread and drink of the cup. For he who eats and drinks, eats and drinks judgment to himself if he does not judge the body rightly.

He warns them to examine their conduct and avoid the judgment and condemnation that comes with the behavior they have been involved in.

"Judging the body" can mean:

- Discerning or understanding that the communion represents the Lord's body, and to take the elements that represent the Lord's body in an improper way is an offense against the body these elements represent.
- Discerning the nature of the church (the body) as a loving and holy fellowship. To act improperly in or against those is an offense against the head of the body: Jesus Christ.

Either way, taking communion unworthily is an offense to God in Christ, as well as His church.

> Vs. 30 – For this reason many among you are weak and sick, and a number sleep.

In that time the displeasure of God for this offense seemed to be manifested by illness and death in the church. These people had gifts of healings but because of their conduct, their gifts were not working, many were struck with illness and death.

> Vs. 31-32 – But if we judged ourselves rightly, we would not be judged. But when we are judged, we are disciplined by the Lord so that we will not be condemned along with the world.

If they conducted themselves properly then God would not punish them. However, if they are being punished, they should submit to it because God ultimately wants to save their souls.

> Vs. 33-34 – So then, my brethren, when you come together to eat, wait for one another. If anyone is hungry, let him eat at home, so that you will not come together for judgment. The remaining matters I will arrange when I come.

Paul does not abolish the love feast, he merely gives instructions concerning it. If you can't wait for each other, eat at home and avoid condemnation and punishment. Keep the love feast, just make sure you do it properly by keeping the love in the love feast.

Summary

A few lessons about this passage:

1. In order to be "a church" we must follow the instructions for worship, organization, work, etc. outlined in the New Testament. Christians who gather together in one spot do not automatically constitute "a church or congregation."

2. It is possible to take communion in an unworthy manner today by acting improperly towards Jesus and His body, the church. To proclaim the Lord's death as a silent witness by taking communion, but giving a witness of disbelief by your actions and words each day is to bring judgment on yourself. Communion is a silent way to say, "I believe," your lifestyle the rest of the week needs to match your witness on Sunday. Would someone believe that you have taken communion on Sunday by the way you act on Monday?

3. Acting unworthily towards the body of Jesus. The Corinthians were judged because they treated their brethren badly and acted badly in the assembly. How can we refuse to support the church, not serve the church, speak badly about the church, neglect our responsibilities in the church, act in a disrespectful way at church (bad speech, practice our bad habits, act foolishly during worship) – and then take communion? Perhaps our lives would go better in our day if we judged the body rightly.

4. Communion is the true "love feast." Remember that they ate together to signify that they were one body, that they loved each other and that they were all growing in Christ. I believe it is permissible to eat together in the building because they did it then; however, let's remember that their love feast was there to prepare them for the true love feast which was communion. Let's have our fellowship dinners, but let's remember that they should be about love, sharing and growth – not just about convenience and food.

11.
MANY MEMBERS - ONE BODY

I CORINTHIANS 12:12

I have mentioned before that I Corinthians is a letter that deals exclusively with church related issues and problems. It could be subtitled "Answers to common problems in the church." In chapter 12 Paul uses a figure to describe what the church is like and how it functions. The figure he uses is that of the human body.

In this chapter I'd like to review some reasons why the body is the perfect figure to represent the church.

> Vs. 12 – For even as the body is one and yet has many members, and all the members of the body, though they are many, are one body, so also is Christ.

Why "body" for church

In the Bible there are over 50 "figures" used to refer to the church, or God's people. Here are a few examples of these:

- City of the living God – Hebrews 12:22

- God's building – I Corinthians 3:9

- Holy mountain – Zechariah 8:3

In each instance the figure represents some aspect or feature of the church that God was trying to accentuate. When the Holy Spirit uses the human body as a figure for the church He is trying to convey three particular things about the church not possible with any other imagery:

1. Glory of the church

In Ephesian 5:27 Paul says that Jesus wishes to present to God the "glorious church." No other figure quite captures the gloriousness of the church than the figure of the human body. In Genesis we read that God creates time, space, matter, and builds on these to fashion the form of the earth and the heavenly bodies. Scientists are still being amazed by the wonders yet discovered under the seas, and estimate that there are billions of stars and heavenly bodies in the universe. And yet, as wonderful and awe-inspiring as those are, God then created living creatures that surpassed these in the fact that they could perceive themselves, and actually interact with the environment (no star or planet can do this).

As overwhelming as the number of stars is, the life experienced by animate creatures such as animals and birds are still more wondrous than a zillion inanimate stars. But then, as a crowning act, God created a being that was made in His own image. Animals could perceive themselves and others, but God created a being that could perceive God and relate to the creator.

For all of these other things, the stars, the earth, the vegetation, the animals, God merely spoke and they came into existence. But when it came to the being that was to exist in the image of God, the one who could see the stars and rule over the animals, God specifically formed a body.

The human body was a unique and separate act of creation, and for this reason only after the human body was created did God say, "It is very good" (Genesis 1:31). So far as the book of Genesis is concerned, the human body rests at the apex of God's creation. When we look at things that were created, the human body is the very best of what God has done. So good, in fact, that God Himself inhabited one!

My point here is that in order to signify how glorious, how marvelous is this thing called the church, God uses the figure of the human body to describe it. The human body is His most glorious creation in the natural world, a thing we can see and appreciate, and so God uses this image to describe His most glorious creation in the spiritual world: the church.

He uses the human body to explain the glory and...

2. The unity of the church

Now when I use the word unity I don't mean conformity. Conformity is for ball bearings. Each one is designed and manufactured to look, feel and weigh exactly the same. No deviations, no changes and no variations. When I use the word unity, I'm referring to a quality that the church possesses. The way that each of its parts work together perfectly in order to make the entire unit function and grow.

Paul points out this wonderful quality of the church by comparing it to the human body that is infinitely complex but functions in such a way that each part, no matter how small or great, is connected to all the other parts, and has a very specific duty that contributes to the overall well being of that body.

These ideas are brought out in several epistles:

- In Romans 12:4-5 Paul contrasts the interconnectedness and diversity of the body.

- In I Corinthians 12:12-19 he demonstrates the cooperative nature of the body where every part is in harmony, not in competition with, every other part; and every part is necessary.

- In Ephesians 4:16 Paul shows that not only are the parts connected and necessary, but each part makes a very specific contribution to the growth of the body.

The church described in the New Testament is united, and by using the human body as a figure to represent it, the Holy Spirit is able to clearly demonstrate what unity means.

- Interconnectedness – each member is related, through faith in Christ and hope of salvation, to every other member. Everyone equally shares a history of being saved and a future of eternal life with God. This is how we are connected.

- Diversity – although each is connected, there is room for individuality. Not everyone thinks, acts and understands in the same way or at the same pace. Not every organ and member of a human body looks the same or grows at the same rate, but it is still part of the body. In the same way, not every member of the church looks, acts or grows at the same pace but nevertheless, it belongs in the church.

- Function – there is a role for every member of the church, and each role is necessary for the overall growth and well being of the church.

You do not produce unity by forcing everyone to think, act and grow exactly the same way. That is conformity and manipulation. This is what Paul is arguing against. He says that unity is created in the following ways:

- Celebrating our interconnectedness. Worship's horizontal purpose is the celebration of our interconnectedness in Christ (I Corinthians 10: 16-17).

- Accepting each other's diversity within the body (Romans 14:3-4). Denouncing our differences destroys unity. We have to guard against false teachings and those who cause division, but simply looking different or having a different opinion does not make one a heretic.

- Promoting the value of each other's contribution to the whole. "Therefore encourage one another and build up one another..." (1 Thessalonians 5:11). The fastest way to build up the body is by praising your brother's work.

The body is the perfect symbol to represent the dynamic element of unity present within the church.

1. The position of Christ

The church is related to, united to and connected to the divine savior Jesus Christ, the Son of God. He is the living Lord and so any symbol or figure used to represent an intricate part of His nature must itself be alive, and alive with the same life as Jesus. In other places the church is referred to in various ways:

- As a city – Hebrews 12:22

- As a flock – Ezekiel 34:15

- As a temple or building – I Corinthians 3:9

- As a portion – Deuteronomy 32:9

These and many others signify various aspects of the Lord's relationship with His people, but only in the use of the body as a figure do we clearly see the three main truths regarding God's position in the church:

1. He is the head of the church
– Colossians 1:18

There is but one leader of the church and that is Jesus Christ. That each human body has one head is easily seen and accepted. This natural phenomenon is an absolutely perfect reflection of the natural position of Jesus Christ with His church. Although there are many diverse members with many functions, there is clearly only one head and that position is not shared or challenged by any of the members.

2. He is the nourisher of the church
– Colossians 2:19

Science explains to us that the control center for the body is the brain contained in the head, and it directs our thoughts, feelings, body functions and reactions.

All are controlled and initiated by the brain. We could lose almost every organ and member of our body and continue to be "alive" or "conscious" if the brain remains healthy. But, if our brain is damaged, the entire body goes to waste.

What a perfect analogy for the position of Christ and His church. He provides everything we need for life as His body, the church, and without Him the church would not function. We can lose members, damage different parts, but the body itself continues to live because Christ, the head, continues to live.

Jesus Himself alluded to this when He said, "I am the vine, you are the branches; he who abides in me, and I in him, he bears much fruit; for apart from me you can do nothing" (John 15:5). In this passage He is referring to His headship of the church.

3. He is united to the church
– Ephesians 4:15-16

Think about this now:

- Jesus has always existed – John 1:1

- The church has not always existed because it is made up of humans, and humans came into existence with Adam – Genesis 1:27

- Now, the church is united to Christ and has become part of His being – John 17:22-23

I don't claim to understand completely the dynamics of our relationship with the Lord, but the head on a human body is not detachable – it is part of the body, it is one with the body. The use of the body as a figure for the church can also reveal to us that God so loved us that He attached us into the Godhead through Jesus Christ.

This concept could not have been conveyed in any other way except by using the human body as a mirror of what took place in the Godhead. We see in this that Jesus, through His incarnation, resurrection and ascension, eternally attaching the church to Himself and the Godhead.

Summary

There is symmetry in the Bible. No wasted words or notions. Every idea and symbol carefully plotted to reveal the marvelous plan of God to save man through Jesus Christ.

The creation of the human body was God's greatest revealed achievement, and it is fitting that the human body also be used as a figure for God's final revealed creation: the church of Christ.

Through this symbol God is able to reveal to human eyes and minds:

- The glory of His church

- The unity of His church

- The relationship of His church to Himself (not only are we one with Christ but he has condescended to be one with us)

One other idea conveyed by the use of the body that is less obvious at first glance:

- Only the body, the human body is alive with "human" life.

  - Animals no matter how powerful

  - Stars no matter how numerous

  - Water no matter how deep

  Do not share the consciousness of life that is evident only in human life.

- Only human bodies are "human." In the same way, only the body of Christ is alive spiritually.

  - Religion, no matter how zealous or old

  - Philosophy, no matter how complex

  Do not have the "life" that only the church/the body of Christ has.

- Only that which is attached to God through Christ has the life that God gives. All other bodies have movement, have substance – but they don't have the spiritual, divine life that the "body of Christ" has.

This is why we invite all people to become members of the only body that has divine life – the church of Christ. (Romans 16:16; Galatians 3:25-26).

12.
THE CHARACTER OF LOVE
I CORINTHIANS 13:1-13

As we study the chapters leading up to chapter 13 we can see that this Corinthian congregation has its share of problems.

- Division because of pride and competition.

- Ungrateful attitude toward the ones who originally brought them to Christ.

- Sexual immorality.

- Lawsuits and arguments.

- Divorce problems.

- Judging each other, complaining.

- Poor behavior during worship.

- Lack of unity.

Normally, it would take a library of books to deal with each of these issues, give advice on how to correct these problems and avoid them in the future. But Paul summarizes the solution to these problems in just a few verses of chapter 13.

The remedy, he says, for all of their problems is to begin to cultivate the character of love, and in doing so these problems will evaporate. I want us to examine this character of love.

The Character of Love – 13:1-8

In describing the character of love, Paul reveals three important elements about love that makes it so valuable to a Christian.

1. Love is essential

> Vs. 1-3 – If I speak with the tongues of men and of angels, but do not have love, I have become a noisy gong or a clanging cymbal. If I have the gift of prophecy, and know all mysteries and all knowledge; and if I have all faith, so as to remove mountains, but do not have love, I am nothing. And if I give all my possessions to feed the poor, and if I surrender my body to be burned, but do not have love, it profits me nothing.

You can have the trappings of religion, even display the dynamic signs, but if you don't love you are missing the essence of what Christianity is all about (i.e. A flashy car with no motor is lovely to look at but will not take you anywhere).

He uses three examples to demonstrate that love is essential in Christianity. Even if one displays miraculous signs but doesn't love – his signs point to nothing, they are useless. Signs are to verify that God is near, but without love the signs are meaningless (God is not where love is not). Jesus rebuked those who thought that their ability to perform signs was enough (Matthew 7:22-23).

Knowledge, the ability to preach, prophesy or strong faith, these are not substitutes for love. Paul says that the object of teaching, the result of knowledge, the fruit of one's faith is, "love from a pure heart" (1 Timothy 1:5). All of the teaching we receive is to create love in our hearts, and if we don't love, we have obviously not put what we have learned into practice.

Even zeal and generosity are misguided if not motivated by love. People will die for ideals, devote millions to causes that help others, but if they do it because of pride or misguided loyalty, their sacrifice is useless; only giving out of love is honored by God.

God looks into a person's heart and if his power, knowledge and works are not grounded in love, they have no value in the sight of God.

2. Love is visible

> Vs. 4-7 – Love is patient, love is kind and is not jealous; love does not brag and is not arrogant, does not act unbecomingly; it does not seek its own, is not provoked, does not take into account a wrong suffered, does not rejoice in unrighteousness, but rejoices with the truth; bears all things, believes all things, hopes all things, endures all things.

There are some things like power, faith and works which are legitimate if based on unseen love within a person's heart. There are also visible attributes that are unmistakable signs that a person has love:

- Patience – a willingness to bear with other peoples' meanness, weaknesses and offenses without losing a loving attitude.

- Kindness – the doing and saying of good.

- Not jealous – envious of another's blessings; fearful of losing one's blessings.

- Not brag/arrogant – boastful, haughty, proud. Having an unjust measure of self.

- Not act unbecomingly – to be unthoughtful, uncaring.

- Not seek its own – selfishness, self-centered.

- Not provoked – bad temper, over-sensitive.

- Not count wrongs – vengeful; get even attitude (doesn't keep score).

- Rejoice in right – loves to see right done, not wrong.

- Bears all things – capacity to suffer much without complaint (everybody suffers – some complain more).

- Believes all things – not suspicious (not a gullible person, but not overly suspicious).

- Hopes all things – not pessimistic or negative.

- Endures all things – a willingness to bear with injury, inconvenience and hardship without losing one's loving attitude.

When we see these things in people what we see is the character of Christian love. Note that these signs are not based on:

- Emotion – how one feels about something.

- Attraction – like sexual love.

- Mutual interest and service – like the love between friends.

- Relationship – like the love in a family.

No, the love Paul describes here is Christian love, and it is based on a decision not a feeling. We decide that this is going to be the nature of our character...our love, and through the power of the Holy Spirit directed by the word of God – the

Lord will create this love in our hearts a little at a time as each day goes by.

We are not born with this kind of love, we cultivate it through prayer, practice and perseverance in the trials that we experience. This is one of the basic reasons that God allows us to suffer trials, so we can cultivate Christian love.

3. Love is eternal – vs. 8-11

The following is a complicated passage open to various interpretations, but before we get into it we need to understand that Paul is talking about love and he says that its most important feature is that it is eternal (verse 8a: love never fails). The reason for this is that love is God's essential character (God is love – I John 4:8).

Some things we, the church, need for now like prophecy, tongues and knowledge. However, the day will come when these things will no longer be necessary because we will be able to experience fully our relationship with God.

The essence of that experience will not require prophecy or tongues or knowledge; the core of our experience with God will be love. Him loving us and us loving Him, without the need for any assistance through prophecy, miracles or learning. This is the general idea of the passage.

> Vs. 8b – But if there are gifts of prophecy, they will be done away; if there are tongues, they will cease; if there is knowledge, it will be done away.

After he declares the eternal nature of love, he explains that the other elements of Christianity (prophecy, tongues, knowledge) that were experienced in a miraculous way at that time – a little background...

- Some could predict the future or speak directly from God.

- Some could speak in languages they had never learned.

- Others had wisdom and understanding of spiritual matters that they received from God without study or training.

God gave, in a miraculous way, the things that the Bible provides for us today in a natural way. These gifts were necessary for the growth of the church at that time because it did not yet possess the full revelation of God in the Bible.

Paul says that these highly prized gifts (that, at times, caused much pride and division in the hands of sinful people), these gifts would eventually cease.

> Vs. 9-10 – For we know in part and we prophesy in part; but when the perfect comes, the partial will be done away.

He says that these abilities, even though experienced in a miraculous way, don't completely reveal what is to come. This is where the difficulty comes in:

- Some say that the "perfect" that is supposed to come is the full word of God: the complete Bible, and when the complete text of the Bible was finally produced, the miraculous gifts stopped.

- Others argue that the "perfect" is the second coming of Christ. When He comes we will no longer need prophecy, tongues or knowledge in miraculous or natural forms because we will be face to face with Him.

I believe that Paul is referring to the second coming of Christ because this is more in keeping with the rest of the passage. However, this doesn't mean I believe in miraculous tongues, prophecy and knowledge today. Look carefully at what Paul says:

Prophecy, tongues, and knowledge will cease.

I believe that these miraculous powers were given by the laying on of hands of the Apostles and when they died, these powers were no longer available. Their deaths and the death of their disciples (who had power) were within a century of the distribution of the New Testament throughout the church. With the New Testament in hand the church could do all the work previously done by those who possessed these powers. In other words, the New Testament is now the tool by which we accomplish the things that had been done previously through the people who had these miraculous gifts.

When the "perfect" comes, the partial will be done away. To this day we still have partial knowledge, partial prophecy (like it says in verse 9).

Can anyone say they understand perfectly all the information in the Bible? All the spiritual and intellectual implications of every verse?

Can anyone say that they understand all the prophecy in the Bible? Who is the man of lawlessness? What will we be like at resurrection? When will Jesus come?

Even though we have the entire word of God revealed to us, and through it can attain salvation and all godliness – we still only know in part, only understand prophecy in part and will only have complete knowledge when the perfect comes: that is the coming of Jesus Christ.

> Vs. 11-12 – When I was a child, I used to speak like a child, think like a child, reason like a child; when I became a man, I did away with childish things. For now we see in a mirror dimly, but then face to face; now I know in part, but then I will know fully just as I also have been fully known.

Paul uses two analogies to drive home his point:

1. Growing up. Grown-ups put away their childish notions and ideas. They should stop being proud about abilities that are only there to serve them for a time and look forward to the object of their Christian experience: the coming of Christ; and be ready for that by cultivating the character of love.

2. The mirror he talks about is the understanding they have of God reflected in His word. God is not a word, He is a being, but at the moment all they know of Him is what they read; and they don't even understand everything they read. But when Jesus comes, then they won't just read about God, they will be in His presence and will see and know Him as God sees and knows them.

> Vs. 13 – But now faith, hope, love, abide these three; but the greatest of these is love.

Paul goes back to his original point, and that is that love is eternal. Faith brings you to God, hope sustains you while you wait to be in His presence, but love is the actual experience that one will have eternally when Jesus comes to take us to heaven with Him.

He encourages them to realize that love will be the lasting experience of Christianity and not to be proud of or try to hold on to the temporary gifts of prophecy, tongues or knowledge.

Summary

Well we have had to digress a little to explain a complicated passage but I don't want you to miss the essential lesson of this chapter: love is the character of Christians.

- It is the essential quality that confirms sincere faith and legitimate works.

- It is a visible quality that is very different from family or sexual love.

- It is eternal in nature and is the objective towards which our knowledge and faith direct us.

- One day, when Jesus comes, it will be the essence of our experience with God.

Love is the character of Christianity because love is the character of Christ. In this passage you could say that Jesus is patient, Jesus is kind, Jesus is not jealous, does not brag, is not arrogant, etc. We abide in love because Jesus is love and we want to abide in Jesus.

13.
PURPOSE OF PREACHING

I CORINTHIANS 14:1-4

In our study of I Corinthians we need to keep an eye on the big picture in order to properly understand the individual pieces. This letter is one of instruction to a dynamic church with dynamic problems. Among these are:

- They are first generation Christians that have come out of the worst pagan society and practice (some not completely out).

- They possess incredible spiritual gifts: some can heal, others have the ability to speak in tongues, and still others can prophesy and have inspired wisdom and knowledge.

- They have great potential, however, they are constantly fighting for preeminence, position and power using their spiritual gifts in their pursuit of these things.

In answer to their problems Paul encourages them to cultivate the character of Christ-like love in order to neutralize their pride and promote harmony and peace among the group.

In chapter 14, however, he provides them with more practical direction on the proper use and purpose for the gifts they have received, including the gift of preaching.

Terms

Before we go through the passage we need to understand some of the terms Paul uses:

1. Prophecy

- Comes from two words which meant to speak and forth; to speak forth.

- In biblical context it was the speaking forth of the mind of God.

- Throughout the Old and New Testaments prophets not only predicted future events, they also "spoke forth" the mind of God about the past, present and future.

- During biblical times (both Old and New Testament) the prophets spoke directly from God as the Holy Spirit gave them utterance (II Peter 1:21).

- As the Bible was collected and written down into one document, this miraculous ability ceased and was carried out in a natural way by preachers and teachers who used the revelation of God recorded in the Bible.

- The difference between then and now is that the message of the prophet was a direct revelation of the mind of God for the occasion; the message of the modern day preacher or teacher is gathered from the completed revelation contained in the Bible.

2. Tongues

This word comes from the Greek word meaning "a tongue." It has several uses in the Bible depending on context:

- A physical organ of speech (the tongue).

- A language. When you add other endings to this word you get the Greek word for tribe, people or nation.

- The meaning of this word in this chapter is the supernatural ability to speak in a language you have never learned.

4. Revelation

- Something man cannot know through reason or study alone.

- Information only obtainable if God gives it to you.

- Something to happen in the future.

5. Interpretation (as it is used in I Corinthians 14)

- The ability to understand a language you have never learned. It seems that some could only speak unknown languages (tongues), and some could only understand unknown languages (interpretation).

The gifts only worked if there was cooperation between God and the Corinthians, and the Corinthians with one another.

This is a long chapter but Paul lays out his case in the first four verses with the rest of the chapter being an explanation of details and application.

> Vs. 1 – Pursue love, yet desire earnestly spiritual gifts, but especially that you may prophesy.

He does not want to dampen their enthusiasm for spiritual gifts (even though they have been misusing them) but he does want them to get some perspective on their purpose and value (the ability to proclaim/explain God's word). In the hierarchy of gifts he places prophecy at the top as the most useful and valuable. In the next three verses he explains why this is so.

> Vs. 2 – For one who speaks in a tongue does not speak to men but to God; for no one understands, but in his spirit he speaks mysteries.

One who has the gift of tongues does not understand what he is saying (mystery) nor does anyone else (unless there is an interpreter) so the only one who knows what is being said is God because He understands all language (i.e. If I broke out into Chinese all of a sudden and was reciting Psalms 23, I would be amazed and so would you but no one would understand what I'd be saying except God, and Chinese people here, if any).

> Vs. 3 – But one who prophesies speaks to men for edification and exhortation and consolation.

The one, however, who speaks to men in their own language and preaches or teaches God's word so all can understand accomplishes the very purpose that God intended His word and the utterance of it to have. The preaching/prophesying of God's word in a miraculous or natural way promotes:

1. Edification

Literally means to build a home. It is used in the New Testament to describe the building or promotion of spiritual growth in others. This is done by example, teaching or providing strength to those who are weak.

2. Exhortation

Means to "call to one side." Basically to call or urge others to a proper course of conduct, always with the intention of betterment and with an eye to the future (i.e. press on to maturity).

3. Consolation

Comes from the same word as exhortation but with a different purpose. Consolation means to "come along side but with a greater degree of tenderness." The same word is used to refer to the Holy Spirit.

Along with declaring the good news of the gospel in as many ways as possible, the purpose of preaching/teaching, especially pulpit preaching, is well summarized in this one verse. Modern preaching's purpose is to:

- Build up the church by teaching it the whole counsel of God and setting in order the things that are not orderly or functioning in a biblical fashion. This happens through preaching, teaching, organizing, ministries and managing various projects to build a New Testament church.

- Encourage the church as a group and as individuals to do the right thing. This is the hardest part of the work because people don't like to be told what they need to do, and they don't like their sins pointed out to them. More preachers crash here because in doing this part of their work they invoke the anger and resentment of people in the church, and some opt for revenge instead of repentance.

- Comfort and encourage those who are weak because of spiritual immaturity or physical limitations. Weddings, funerals, hospital visits, especially those events that remind us of God's mercy, strength and goodness.

Paul reminds them that these are the kind of things that people need in the church, and the ability to prophesy was the gift that provided these things for the congregation.

Today we don't prophesy from direct revelation about the past, present and future. Today, because we have God's word, we prophesy about the past, present and future so far as it has been revealed to us in the Bible.

- I know the past from the Bible perspective and can use it to instruct the church (I Corinthians 10:11).

- I can comment on our present state using the word as my guide for Christian living (II Timothy 3:16).

- I can look into the future knowing what will happen at the end of the world and how to prepare for that now (I Thessalonians 4:15-18).

Prophecy or preaching remains one of the most important ministries because through it the church continues to be built up, motivated and comforted in times of trouble. Most churches take their preachers for granted until they don't have them anymore.

Summary

In the next chapter, which will continue to focus on this passage, we will take a look at how Paul teaches them to use their various gifts, and how each of them complemented the other in the working out of God's plan for the growth of the church. In the meantime, let us zero in on a couple of important lessons based on what we have covered so far:

1. Pursue love

Pursue means to eagerly follow after or chase after love. Don't just wait for love to happen to you, you must go after it, build it, care for it, find how to establish and reestablish it when it is broken.

In the church we strive to reach high ideals, we expect a lot from each other and so it is easy to be disappointed when people let us down, and even easier to get angry for real or imaginary hurts. For these reasons we need to be proactive in our effort to create a loving attitude with others, and willing to reestablish love with those we are separated from for whatever reasons.

2. Desire earnestly spiritual gifts

Of course, Paul has just said that some gifts would end (inspired prophecy, tongues, etc.) but not all gifts are gone. In Romans 12:6-8 he names gifts and talents that still function in the church today, which are spiritual and given by the Holy Spirit, but are not miraculous:

- Prophecy – ability to preach today

- Service – ministry in its various forms

- Teaching – opportunity and ability to teach others about Christ

- Exhortation – those who encourage and counsel

- Giving – people rarely ask God to give them the ability to give generously to the church whether rich or poor

- Leadership – whether as an elder, deacon or one who manages one of our ministries

- Shows mercy – benevolence work

All of these are gifts God enables us to exercise for the growth of the kingdom. Paul says we need to desire these kinds of things. These things should be the subject of our prayers, not just, "Dear God give me more health, wealth and peace of mind." Our prayers should be "Dear God, give me a gift to exercise in your name for the blessing of others."

3. Purpose of preaching is to make the church grow

Preaching wasn't invented by man; it is God's way to feed the church. Preachers are simply vessels of clay (as Paul says) who hold, for a few moments, the precious living word of God.

The overriding emotion that I have as I do this work is that of unworthiness, and this idea is shared by most preachers I speak to. I have succeeded if I have accurately and lovingly preached only God's word. You are receiving it properly if you respond to the word (not me) in obedience and joy, in comfort and encouragement. Only in this way is God glorified, the church edified and the preaching justified.

14.

ORDER IN WORSHIP

I CORINTHIANS 14:5-40

Previously we studied the opening part of this section that laid out the basic theme for the entire chapter. There are many gifts given by God, but prophecy (preaching/teaching today) is the most important because it is through this gift that God accomplishes three things necessary for the church:

1. Edification – building up the church

2. Exhortation – giving direction

3. Consolation – comforting

This is what the church needs to remain alive and growing. I could add that in another passage Paul also says that preaching is important because it is the manner in which God calls men to be saved (I Corinthians 1:21).

The reason for this reminder was that in this congregation there existed a number of gifted men and women, and Paul had to teach them the true purpose and way to use their gifts. Some were using their gift of preaching to debate and create a following. Others were using their ability to speak in unlearned languages (tongues) to show off.

He begins, therefore, by teaching them the role of the primary gift, and from there moves on to explain the purpose and manner of usage for other gifts in the church.

The secondary theme that summarizes the second part of this chapter is found in verse 40. In public gatherings of Christians for worship the guiding principles for conduct are:

- Propriety – decency, graciousness, honor
- Orderliness – arranged, orderly, opposite of confusion

The instructions he gives in verses 6-38 are those which will guarantee propriety and orderliness in the public assembly, especially among those who are misusing and misunderstanding the gifts of prophecy and tongues.

Purpose of Tongues

He begins by teaching them the two purposes for which the gift of tongues had been given. He has already explained the purposes for the gift of prophecy, now he reviews with them the purposes for the gift of tongues.

1. For Instruction

Tongues was a gift through which the church received some form of instruction, but received it in a supernatural way (rather than simple, natural communication).

> Vs. 6 – But now, brethren, if I come to you speaking in tongues, what will I profit you unless I speak to you either by way of revelation or of knowledge or of prophecy or of teaching?

What good is the foreign language (tongues) I speak unless it instructs you in some manner?

- Revelation – reveal what was until now unknown through divine inspiration.

- Knowledge – ability to accumulate and analyze information accurately.

- Prophecy – speaking God's word concerning the past, present and future.

- Teaching – applying and explaining in practical terms the word of God.

If what I am saying does not serve you in one of these ways, what profit, what good is my speech?

> Vs. 7-8 – Yet even lifeless things, either flute or harp, in producing a sound, if they do not produce a distinction in the tones, how will it be known what is played on the flute or on the harp? For if the bugle produces an indistinct sound, who will prepare himself for battle?

Here Paul compares a language no one understands to different musical instruments. He says that each instrument has a distinct and recognizable sound that helps the listener identify it (i.e. the bugle is effective because its distinctive sound instructs you to prepare for battle).

> Vs. 9-11 – So also you, unless you utter by the tongue speech that is clear, how will it be known what is spoken? For you will be speaking into the air. There are, perhaps, a great many kinds of languages in the world, and no kind is without meaning. If then I do not know the meaning of the language, I will be to the one who speaks like a barbarian, and the one who speaks will be a barbarian to me.

Now he demonstrates that language is the same. Each language has its own "sound" or meaning. Note that he refers to human language (verse 10).

If one understands the meaning or "sound" of that language, then that person receives instruction. However, if people do not understand each others' languages (even if they know each other) it is like speaking to a Barbarian (or a foreigner) – there is no understanding.

Remember that the purpose of tongues is for instruction, so if there is no understanding there is no instruction, and the purpose is defeated.

> Vs. 12-17 – So also you, since you are zealous of spiritual gifts, seek to abound for the edification of the church. Therefore let one who speaks in a tongue pray that he may interpret. For if I pray in a tongue, my spirit prays, but my mind is unfruitful. What is the outcome then? I will pray with the spirit and I will pray with the mind also; I will sing with the spirit and I will sing with the mind also. Otherwise if you bless in the spirit only, how will the one who fills the place of the ungifted say the "Amen" at your giving of thanks, since he does not know what you are saying? For you are giving thanks well enough, but the other person is not edified.

He tells them not to be selfish, their gift needed to edify (or serve) the entire church not just themselves. If they spoke in a tongue that no one (including themselves) understood, they might feel good inwardly that they were doing something special, but no one else was being served by it.

Paul encourages them to seek the complimentary gift of interpretation so that everyone could be blessed by the gift.

> Vs. 18-19 – I thank God, I speak in tongues more than you all; however, in the church I desire to speak five words with my mind so that I may instruct others also, rather than ten thousand words in a tongue.

Paul acknowledges that he possesses the gift of tongues more than they but if there are no interpreters for his tongues, he'd rather speak in their own language so they could understand what he was saying.

So the first purpose for this gift was to provide instruction and to do it in a miraculous way – not just to show off.

2. For a Sign

It was a gift that provided a sign to unbelievers that what was being said was from God.

> Vs. 20-22 – Brethren, do not be children in your thinking; yet in evil be infants, but in your thinking be mature. In the Law it is written, "by men of strange tongues and by the lips of strangers I will speak to this people, and even so they will not listen to me," say the Lord. So then tongues are for a sign, not to those who believe but to unbelievers; but prophecy is for a sign, not to unbelievers but to those who believe.

Paul explains that this miracle was prophesied long ago in connection with the coming of the gospel. It would be a signal that the gospel was being preached. We know that the Apostles were the first to demonstrate it at Pentecost (Acts 2:1-42).

This also explained why this gift faded. It was given as a sign that the promise of the Old Testament had finally arrived. It was a gift more significant to the Jews than the Gentiles since it referred to Old Testament prophecy.

> Vs. 23-25 – Therefore if the whole church assembles together and all speak in tongues, and ungifted men or unbelievers enter, will they not say that you are mad? But if all prophesy, and an unbeliever or an ungifted man enters, he is convicted by all, he is called to account by all; the secrets of his heart are disclosed; and so he will fall on his face and worship God, declaring that God is certainly among you.

Paul creates a scenario where an unbeliever (and one without miraculous gifts) enters a church where all speak tongues but there are no interpreters. In a case like this the unbeliever would not understand, and probably think everyone was crazy because of the confusion. But, if everyone prophesied in a language understood, this would convict and convert the unbeliever.

The equation then is that a tongue plus an interpretation equals a prophecy. Once you have prophecy, tongues and interpretation are not necessary.

Instructions for Orderly Worship

Having explained the true purposes for the gifts (tongues/interpretation), Paul now goes on to explain how orderly worship should be conducted.

> Vs. 26 – What is the outcome then, brethren? When you assemble, each one has a psalm, has a teaching, has a revelation, has a tongue, has an interpretation. Let all things be done for edification.

Make sure that you are using your gift for the right purpose: to bless and build up the assembly.

> Vs. 27-35 – If anyone speaks in a tongue, it should be by two or at the most three, and each in turn, and one must interpret; but if there is no interpreter, he must keep silent in the church; and let him speak to himself and to God. Let two or three prophets speak, and let the others pass judgment. But if a revelation is made to another who is seated, the first one must keep silent. For you can all prophesy one by one, so that all may learn and all may be exhorted; and the spirits of prophets are subject to prophets; for God is not a God of confusion but of peace, as in all the churches of the saints. The women are to keep silent in the churches; for they are not permitted to speak, but are to subject themselves, just as the Law also says. If they desire to learn anything, let them ask their own husbands at home; for it is improper for a woman to speak in church.

Some basic rules of order in public worship:

1. Those who speak tongues should do it one at a time and no more than three with this gift should exercise it at one time.

   - After each speaks, the interpretation should be made by one person. It seems that the gift of interpretation was such that one person could interpret many kinds of tongues.

2. If no one can interpret, then this gift should not be used publicly since no one is edified. The individual can only express it privately.

3. In the same way prophets need to take turns speaking, and when they are, what they say is to be judged (discerned) by the other prophets who have the gift of discernment or knowledge.

   - Preachers and teachers took turns in on-going preaching and teaching cycle, and were subject to each others' correction for the edification of the church and guarantee of correct doctrine.

   - Today we have the preachers and teachers teach at appointed times and they are subject to correction by each other, the elders and those in the congregation who have Bible knowledge.

4. Give the place to speak to the one that has a word from the Lord and do not all talk at the same time.

- Every prophet has a chance to speak but there must be orderliness in the Lord's church whenever it meets (no shouting each other down).

5. Women, regardless of their gifts (whether they can speak in tongues, interpret or prophesy) are not permitted to exercise their gifts in the public assembly.

- The Bible describes women who had gifts (Philip's daughters all prophesied) but Paul instructs them not to use them in the public assembly. It is improper to do so.

- Gifts can be used with unbelievers (Aquila and Priscilla), children (Timothy) or other women (Lydia) but not in mixed public assembly.

> Vs. 36-38 – Was it from you that the word of God first went forth? Or has it come to you only? If anyone thinks he is a prophet or spiritual, let him recognize that the things which I write to you are the Lord's commandment. But if anyone does not recognize this, he is not recognized.

Paul anticipates protest over the things he has just instructed, and reminds them of the source of his own authority in these matters: the Lord Himself.

These instructions are not merely suggestions, they are commandments from the Lord. If one ignores these in worship then the worship is ignored by God. (I Timothy 2:11-15 – eternal vs. cultural basis for teaching.)

> Vs. 39-40 – Therefore, my brethren, desire earnestly to prophesy, and do not forbid to speak in tongues. But all things must be done properly and in an orderly manner.

A summary statement:

- Tongues are not the preeminent gift and are the cause of problems, but this is not a reason to forbid their use. Use them but do so in a proper way.

- Make sure everything is done in a proper and orderly way (meaning according to the instruction guide).

Summary

We do not possess the miraculous gifts of tongues, interpretation, inspired prophecy, discernment or revelation today. However, we can still accomplish the same goals that these gifts helped the early church to achieve.

- Edification – build up

- Exhortation – direct

- Encouragement – comfort

- Conviction – of sin

- Conversion – to Christ

Today we have the word of God revealed and recorded in the Bible. We also have preachers, teachers, elders, deacons and saints who through the ministry of this word:

1. Edify the church

> And He gave some as apostles, some as prophets, and some as evangelists and teachers for the equipping of the saints for the work of service, to the building up of the body of Christ.
> - Ephesians 4:12

2. Direct the church

> Every scripture is inspired by God and profitable for teaching, reproof, for correction and training in righteousness so the man of God may be adequate, equipped for every good work.
> - II Timothy 3:16

3. Comfort the church

> Comfort each other with these words.
> - I Thessalonians 4:18

4. Convict sinners

> They were pierced to the heart.
> - Acts 2:37

5. Bring souls to Christ

> I am not ashamed...these things not done by miracles but by preaching the word.
> - Romans 1:16

The miraculous gifts are gone but in their place we have the word of God that empowers us to accomplish the very same objectives. And today we also have the same responsibility to conduct our assemblies in an orderly and decent fashion.

We do this with reverent behavior and modest dress (not just sexual concept of dressing but respectful dressing).

We do this by following Paul's instructions.

- The preachers and teachers take turns in class and in the pulpit to minister the word.

- Different teachers are used at different times.

- Those who oversee and those who have Bible knowledge examine carefully what is taught.

- The women exercise their talents in a proper way and proper time.

- All is done in a respectful and orderly fashion.

- Finally, we never allow a meeting time to pass without offering the opportunity for the convicted of sin or convinced by the gospel to come before the assembly to acknowledge this and request prayer or baptism.

We do all of this how? Through miracles? No. Through the preaching and teaching of God's word.

15.

CONCERNING THE COLLECTION

I CORINTHIANS 16:1-24

In this final chapter of the I Corinthians letter, Paul reviews several matters and leaves several words of encouragement to his readers:

- To treat young and inexperienced men with honor and be gentle with them.

- To look forward to the visit of Apollos, another preacher who was a mature teacher.

- To be careful of their faith, be alert against sinfulness and division, and also treat each other with love.

- To respect the ones who lead in supporting mission work and benevolence, and see these types of people as leaders in the church.

- He also gives a variety of greetings to various individuals in the church and offers a blessing on the church.

At the beginning of the chapter, however, he talks about a "special collection" and the details surrounding it. Much of our information about giving in church comes from this reference, so I'd like to focus in on this for this chapter.

The Collection for the Saints – 16:1-9

> Vs. 1 – Now concerning the collection for the saints, as I directed the churches of Galatia, so do you also.

We're not sure which collection Paul is talking about here. In Acts 11:27 there was a special collection on behalf of those in Jerusalem for the poor, but in Acts 12:25 the Bible says that Paul completed this mission and turned the money over to the elders in Jerusalem. In other passages Paul does promise to care for the poor (Romans 15:25; II Corinthians 8-9) and this could be an on-going effort with Paul. In any case, this was a special collection and both Paul and the Corinthians knew about it, and so no further details are given here.

> Vs. 2-4 – On the first day of every week each one of you is to put aside and save, as he may prosper, so that no collections be made when I come. When I arrive, whomever you may approve, I will send them with letters to carry your gift to Jerusalem; and if it is fitting for me to go also, they will go with me.

Here Paul gives the details on how he wants this special collection to be organized.

1. "On the first day" refers to the Lord's Day (Sunday), which was the day that the early Christians met for worship.

2. Each first day each one had to set aside what he had allotted for this special collection.

3. When he came, he wanted no collection to be made; the special collection should have been taken up before his arrival (he explains later that this would be to avoid embarrassment).

4. He himself will not handle the money, but will accompany whoever is appointed to carry it, along with letters of introduction and explanation to its final destination.

5. He also encourages them to give according to their prosperity, according to their own particular wealth.

We find out in II Corinthians that those brethren didn't follow through on this teaching and Paul had to encourage them to finish the good work they had begun in this matter (II Corinthians 8).

From this passage we model the way that we collect money not only for special works but also for our everyday work of the church. From this example we have a pattern of several things:

1. They met regularly on the first day of the week. In Acts 20:7 we see that this pattern was established early and blessed by the Apostles. This is why we do it also.

2. They contributed for the work of the church. The Corinthians were no strangers to giving as a regular feature of their assemblies. Paul, in this passage, gives special instructions about a special need and this is why he insists that at his appearing no collection be made. But early church historians (Pliny) write that the church regularly took up offerings during their weekly Sunday meetings. The New Testament example of this being done here is confirmed by others who lived and wrote about those times.

3. They were concerned about quantity of giving as well as orderliness in the handling of the money. Paul encourages giving in proportion to prosperity. You can't give what you haven't got, but you can give a portion of what you do have and that's the part God is interested in. We also see the care he gives in making

sure that the money is accounted for by people who are trustworthy and that it is used for what it was intended for.

In the churches of Christ one of our guiding principles is that in order to be the church of the Bible, we needed to do things according to Bible teaching. It is important to be the church of the Bible because the Bible says this is the only church saved. Now the Bible "teaches" us in a variety of ways:

- It gives us a clear command or instruction of what we should or should not do and how, when, where, etc. to do it (i.e. when and how and why to do the Lord's Supper, how to respond to the gospel, and who should be elders, etc.).

- It provides examples of the Apostles and the early church living the Christian life and carrying out the Lord's will. Here we can emulate or follow their example in attitude, work and teaching (i.e. we have no command that everyone take bread and wine at communion – we have example).

- It allows us to draw certain conclusions based on information it provides.

  - That there was always two or more elders for each congregation because every time elders are mentioned in the New Testament, the Bible mentions that there were two or more for each congregation. From this we can reason (use our heads) that plurality of elders is the biblical way of doing things.

- o No example of "pastoral system" where one man is the leader of one or more congregations as is the case in many churches. Not found anywhere in the New Testament.

So when we try to figure out how or when or why to do something or other, these are the principles that guide us. These are the ways that we figure out what the Bible is saying:

- Is there a command in the Bible for this and if so, what is it?

- Can we find any examples of Apostles or churches doing this with approval in the Bible?

- Can we logically infer or deduce that this is what the Apostles or early church did in those circumstances from the information we have?

These are the ways we come to understand how to be the church the Bible describes.

There is another less authoritative and less exact way and that is to study what early church historians say about early church activity and teaching. This is usually used to confirm or clarify information we already have in the Bible (i.e. they met on Sunday, had communion, only used vocal music).

The reason I've said all of this is for the following. When it comes to the collection, we arrive at doing what we do, the way we do it, based on this approach (command, example, inference) that is referred to as our hermeneutic (or method) by which we interpret the Bible. Let's apply these rules:

1. There is no direct command to make a collection for the regular work of the church.

2. There is, however, an example of an Apostle and the church meeting on the first day of the week, every week, for worship (I Corinthians 16, Acts 20:7).

    a. Also an example of money being collected and reason for it (I Corinthians 10).

3. We can infer that the church regularly collected money because Paul and others regularly received money to help the poor and those in ministry (Acts 12:25; II Corinthians 8:1-2).

4. In addition to this, early church historians confirm that Christians met each Sunday for worship, and this included singing, communion, teaching and preaching, prayer and the taking up of a collection for the work of the church. We have early church historians confirming what we have examples of and inference for in the New Testament.

We don't need a direct command in order to pattern our behavior and attitudes. An Apostolic example, along with support inferences are sufficient to guide our actions so we can confidently say that what we do and how we do it are according to God's word.

So each week we put aside a portion from what we have, and on Sunday when we meet, we collect it and invest it in the Lord's work in a wise and orderly manner. That's the Bible way!

Summary

How and when we collect the money for the work of the church is not necessarily the most important issue in our faith. But Jesus said that if we are faithful in little things (like an orderly way of collecting and handling the offering) we can be trusted with greater things (the saving of souls).

An interesting feature of this study is how we learn what the Bible teaches on various things, whether it be how to handle money or how to go to heaven. The approach is always the same. When we want to know what the Bible says we need to see what it commands, what it demonstrates and to what conclusion it guides our thinking.

When it comes to salvation we have an overwhelming amount of information in each area. For example:

- The Bible plainly commands what is necessary to be saved (Mark 16:16; Acts 2:38).

- It provides many examples of people who were being saved and what they did to arrive at this (Acts 2:40-42; 47).

- We read stories about people who were searching for salvation and the things that happened to them in this search. These, then, form our conclusions about what is necessary (i.e. the jailer – Acts 16:30-34).

Historians confirm that this is how early converts were made. When we are searching for the same kind of answers for our own souls the Bible provides the commands, examples and inferences we need to guide our response.

So what does the Bible – not the church of Christ – say that we must do to be saved?

- We need to believe in Jesus and confess His name (Matthew 10:32-33; Mark 16:16).

- We need to repent of our sins and be immersed (baptized) in His name for our sins to be forgiven, and for our hearts to receive the Holy Spirit (Matthew 28:18-20; Acts 2:37-42).

16.
VICTORY IN JESUS – PART 1

I CORINTHIANS 15:1-58

The gospel writers describe the events leading up to and including Jesus' resurrection, but do not mention ours very much. This is left to the writers of the epistles. No one discusses this subject in more detail than the Apostle Paul in the first letter to the Corinthian church. In this chapter, therefore, we will review a passage that not only talks about Jesus' resurrection, but also gives us a glimpse of what ours will be like as well.

Death and the Unbeliever

In order to speak about the resurrection we must first discuss the phenomena of death itself. Death, we ignore it until it happens to someone near; then, and only then, does it become real, life changing and powerful. It is when death strikes close to home that we begin to have a real sense of time. The idea that we have only so much time and no more.

Men have struggled with the reality of death in different ways (i.e. the Greek philosophers thought that the best way to deal with the inevitable fact of death was to take control of it yourself by committing suicide; this was the noble or enlightened way to go).

There are many superstitions, ideas, ceremonies and philosophies to help people deal with the reality and pain of death. Paul sums up the non-believer's feelings about death in I Thessalonians 4:13, "but we do not want you to be uniformed, brethren, about those who are asleep, that you may not grieve, as do the rest who have no hope." In those days, like today, when it came to death, unbelievers had no knowledge and no hope. All they knew was: everyone was subject to death, no one ever conquered death, and the only thing one could do was grieve. This was the condition of man until Jesus Christ.

Jesus Christ and Death

Jesus Christ dealt with death in a way that no one had ever done before or since.

- It was the first time someone claimed openly to have power over death (Matthew 28:18).

- It was the first time someone foretold of His own death and subsequent bodily resurrection, and then accomplish it before witnesses.

> The Jews then said to Him, "What sign do You show us as your authority for doing these things?" Jesus answered them, "Destroy this temple, and in three days I will raise it up." The Jews then said, "It took forty-six years to build this temple and will You raise it up in three days? But He was speaking of the temple of His body. So when He was raised from the dead, His disciples remembered that He said this; and they believed the Scripture and the word which Jesus had spoken.
> - John 2:18-22

Most significantly for us, it was the first time such a leader promised to His disciples a similar resurrection from the dead.

> This is the will of Him who sent Me, that of all that He has given Me I lose nothing, but raise it up on the last day. "For this is the will of My father, that everyone who beholds the Son and believes in Him will have eternal life, and I Myself will raise him up on the last day.
> - John 6:39-40

It is this resurrection that I wish to focus on in our study of I Corinthians 15. In it, Paul not only teaches about the reality of Christ's resurrection, but what it has accomplished for the

Corinthians: the possibility of their own resurrection, and ours as well.

Paul's Teaching on our Resurrection

Background on Corinthian letter:

Among other problems in Corinth, it seems that some were maintaining Greek ideas about the immortality of the soul:

- That after death the soul escaped from the body to be absorbed into the divine or to continue some shadowy existence in the underworld.

- To Greeks, physical (conscious) resurrection was impossible (Paul was scoffed at in Athens for even suggesting it, Acts17:32).

Greeks who had become Christians were hanging on and circulating these ideas in the church, and so Paul responds to them by giving more details concerning Christ's resurrection and the eventual resurrection of all believers.

Christs Resurrection

15:1-11 – Now I make known to you, brethren, the gospel which I preached to you, which also you received, in which also you stand, by which also you are saved, if you hold fast the word which I preached to you, unless you believed in vain. For I delivered to you as of first importance what I also received, that Christ died for our sins according to the Scriptures, and that He was buried, and that He was raised on the third day according to the Scriptures, and that He appeared to Cephas, then to the twelve. After that He appeared to more than five hundred brethren at one time, most of whom remain until now, but some have fallen asleep; then He appeared to James, then to all the apostles; and last of all, as to one untimely born, He appeared to me also. For I am the least of the apostles, and not fit to be called an apostle, because I persecuted the church of God. But by the grace of God I am what I am, and His grace toward me did not prove vain; but I labored even more than all of them, yet not I, but the grace of God with me. Whether then it was I or they, so we preach and so you believed.

In this passage Paul re-establishes the fact that Jesus Christ did in fact rise from the dead, and this event was witnessed by numerous people who were still alive at that time and could substantiate his claim. He also re-affirms the idea that the resurrection of Jesus is the basis of the gospel which he and the other Apostles preached, and the rock upon which their salvation was based.

Resurrection of the saints

In the next section Paul deals with the resurrection of believers.

Deals with doubters

He begins by dealing with the logical conclusions that come from doubting the possibility of resurrection. Seven things happen when you doubt:

> Vs. 12-13 – Now if Christ is preached, that He has been raised from the dead, how do some among you say that there is no resurrection of the dead? But if there is no resurrection of the dead, not even Christ has been raised.

If resurrection from the dead is impossible then even Christ is not raised.

> Vs. 14a – And if Christ has not been raised, then our preaching is vain

If Christ is not raised then their preaching is worthless because that's the core of it.

> Vs. 14b – Your faith also is vain.

If Christ is not raised, your faith is for nothing because that is what you hope for.

> Vs. 15 – Moreover we are even found to be false witnesses of God, because we testified against God that

> He raised Christ, who He did not raise, if in fact the dead are not raised.

If Christ is not raised we are liars because we have declared that God raised Him.

> Vs. 16-17 – For if the dead are not raised, not even Christ has been raised; and if Christ has not been raised, your faith is worthless; you are still in your sins.

If there is no resurrection you are still guilty of sin and condemned. Why? An un-risen Christ means that He is guilty of sin. If this be so, then death still holds Him, and He cannot be a perfect sin offering for us.

> Vs. 18 –Then those also who have fallen asleep in Christ have perished.

If Christ is not raised, neither will we be, and so we are without hope just like the pagans.

> Vs. 19 – If we have hoped in Christ in this life only, we are of all men most to be pitied.

If Christ is still in the grave, Christians are to be pitied because their entire lives and hopes are based on illusion.

Denying the resurrection of Christ has disastrous consequences for believers. If Christ is not raised then neither are we, and our faith and religion are worthless. We expect scoffers and non-believers to deny the resurrection, they always have. But for those who call themselves Christians or disciples to do so is foolish and dangerous.

After having addressed the doubters, Paul moves on to speak to and encourage those who do believe in the resurrection, and provide them with more information on this vital topic.

The truth about what to expect

> Vs. 20 – But now Christ has been raised from the dead, the first fruits of those who are asleep.

Christ has been raised from the dead, and this fact witnessed by over 500 people (I Corinthians 15:6). His resurrection, however, is not like that of Lazarus, His friend, or Jairus' daughter who were miraculously brought back to life but eventually had to face death again. His is a glorious resurrection where He will NEVER face death again; this is the type of resurrection we are to look forward to. In addition to this, Jesus' resurrection is the beginning of many other resurrections (Lazarus' resurrection didn't start others). Jesus' resurrection, however, is like the beginning of a harvest: the first fruit is a sign that the rest is ready.

Paul explains how Jesus accomplishes this resurrection, and the procedure it will follow.

He describes how both death and life come into being.

> Vs. 21-22 – For since by a man came death, by a man also came the resurrection of the dead. For as in Adam all die, so also in Christ all will be made alive.

Death, he says, comes through Adam and all who share in his nature. Adam sinned, and death entered as a consequence of sin and spread to all men.

Eternal life comes through Christ and all who share in His nature. Jesus offers forgiveness for sins which removes the penalty of death and provides access to life.

> For the wages of sin is death, but the free gift of God is eternal life in Christ Jesus our Lord.
> - Romans 6:23

And so, death (physical and spiritual) comes through Adam and his sin. Life (eternal and spiritual) comes through faith and union with Christ.

The procedure of resurrection

Here, Paul describes how the resurrection will take place.

1. Christ resurrects first – vs. 23a

2. Believers will resurrect at Jesus' return – vs. 23b

This resurrection will be in conjunction with three other events:

1. The destruction of the wicked – vs. 24-25; II Thessalonians 1:7-8

2. The destruction of death for both the wicked and the just by the power of resurrection – vs. 26

3. The reintegration of man and the Godhead – vs. 27-28

Re-integration of Godhead

Each person in the Godhead has, within the history of mankind, operated in a special way in order to accomplish man's resurrection.

God the Father has initiated the work of salvation by sending the Son. The Son didn't send the Father, the Father sent the Son. God the Son has revealed the Father and His plan to save mankind. The Son has also executed the plan. This is why He came. God the Holy Spirit has maintained the creation after the fall, and empowered the church in its work of preaching the gospel and remaining faithful until the Son returns.

Now, at the resurrection none of the persons in the Godhead will need to exercise a separate ministry on behalf of man's salvation since it will have been completed; resurrection is the last step. The Godhead will be in perfect union with the saints without various roles to accomplish salvation.

Paul says that when the last step of the Father's plan, carried out by the Son, powered by the Spirit, is completed (that being our glorious resurrection), the wicked will be punished, death will be defeated, and the Godhead and man will be re-integrated in perfect union.

This is the "end game" of salvation. That we, the resurrected, become part of the Godhead!

> For this reason I endure all things for the sake of those who are chosen, so that they also may obtain the salvation which is in Christ Jesus and with it eternal glory. It is a trustworthy statement; For if we died with Him, we will also live with Him; If we endure, we will also reign with Him; If we deny Him, He also will deny us.
> - II Timothy 2:10-12

Summary

Paul silences the doubters by reestablishing the fact that Jesus experienced a bodily resurrection witnessed by hundreds of faithful brethren; they shouldn't doubt this fact. He explains that this is a most significant fact in the Christian faith because our hope for forgiveness, resurrection and eternal life are based upon it. Without the resurrection,

Christianity is foolish. He begins to describe the process of our resurrection.

Death comes through sin (the problem in the first place). The first resurrection begins with Jesus who is without sin. Believers will be resurrected when Jesus returns, and that resurrection will be accomplished by:

1. The final judgment and destruction of the wicked.

2. The final destruction of death itself.

3. The final unification of God and man.

17.
VICTORY IN JESUS – PART 2

I CORINTHIANS 15:1-58

Paul is reminding the church about the actual physical resurrection of Jesus. Greek Christians were hanging on to teachings that doubted the possibility of physical resurrection. Paul tells them several things in I Corinthians 15:1-28:

- Without Jesus' resurrection their faith and hope for forgiveness as well as their hope for resurrection and eternal life was foolish.

- He reviews with them the details of Jesus' resurrection and the confirmation of this fact by witnesses still alive at the writing of his letter.

- He then goes on to describe the order and process of the resurrection of the saints.

  o Jesus is raised first.

  o Believers will be resurrected when Jesus returns. This resurrection will be accompanied by:

    - Destruction of wicked (judgment).

    - Abolishment of death.

    - Unification of God and man: the Godhead and man will become one.

After having explained to believers what to expect, he goes back to address the doubters once again. This section is written as if Paul were addressing two groups simultaneously; speaking to one group then to the other.

Speaks to Doubters – 15:29-34

He challenges the doubters, "If there is no resurrection, answer the following questions."

> Vs. 29 – Otherwise, what will those do who are baptized for the dead? If the dead are not raised at all, why then are they baptized for them?

Why are people preparing for resurrection by being baptized? The way this question is written it could be interpreted two ways:

1. Baptized in order to get benefits for someone already dead (i.e. Mormons). This idea is not in context and not supported by any other biblical doctrine. You cannot be baptized in order to have someone else be forgiven and receive the Holy Spirit. A doctrinal idea suggested by one passage needs to be supported by other passages (i.e. Jesus is the Son of God). Paul could also be referring to a mistaken idea people had at that time.

2. People are responding to the gospel in baptism on the strength of the teaching, example and encouragement of Christians who have already died. This idea is supported and repeated throughout the New Testament.

The point he makes is: why are people preparing for death by being baptized if there is no such thing as resurrection?

> Vs. 30-32 – Why are we also in danger every hour? I affirm, brethren, by the boasting in you which I have in Christ Jesus our Lord, I die daily. If from human motives I fought with wild beasts at Ephesus, what does it profit me? If the dead are not raised, let us eat and drink, for tomorrow we die.

If there is no resurrection, why am I in danger, why do I struggle, why am I attacked for my preaching? Why don't I just enjoy this life if there is no life to come in resurrection?

> Vs. 33-34 – Do not be deceived; "Bad company corrupts good morals." Become sober-minded as you ought, and stop sinning; for some have no knowledge of God. I speak this to your shame.

In these verse Paul rebukes all those who are being carried away by the doubters. They should be ashamed of themselves, as Christians, for even considering such a thing. The "bad company" he refers to here are the doubters who use their doubt as an excuse for sin. People unsure of the resurrection have a difficult time letting go of this world. Doubters rarely sacrifice for Christ, rarely lead and rarely go all out for their faith. He tells them that association with those who doubt and have lower morals than they do will weaken them, not strengthen them.

It is a sin to doubt God's promises, especially after such a great witness given by Jesus and the Apostles. How much more evidence do you need?

Details Concerning the Resurrection Itself

So far we have dealt with the doubters, described the procedure and challenged the doubters once again. Now Paul describes the resurrection itself, referring once again to the believers:

The Nature of the Resurrection – vs. 35-49

> Vs. 35-38 – But someone will say, "How are the dead raised? And with what kind of body do they come?" You fool! That which you sow does not come to life unless it dies; and that which you sow, you do not sow the body which is to be, but a bare grain, perhaps of wheat or of something else. But God gives it a body just as He wished, and to each of the seeds a body of its own.

The doubters have raised the issue of how a dead and rotten body comes back to life. Paul answers by using the comparison of a seed. The seed does not resemble the plant that grows from it. The seed must first be planted, decay in the ground and from this a plant will grow. One comes naturally from the other, but both are totally different from each other.

The analogy, of course, is that a human body is planted in death in the earth, and resurrects a different body all together.

> Vs. 39-44 – All flesh is not the same flesh, but there is one flesh of men, and another flesh of beasts, and another flesh of birds, and another of fish. There are also heavenly bodies and earthly bodies, but the glory of the heavenly is one, and the glory of the earthly is another. There is one glory of the sun, and another glory of the moon, and another glory of the stars; for star differs from star in glory. So also is the resurrection of the dead. It is sown a perishable body, it is raised an imperishable body; it is sown in dishonor, it is raised in glory; it is sown in weakness, it is raised in power; it is sown a natural body, it is raised a spiritual body. If there is a natural body, there is also a spiritual body.

Paul explains how God has created different qualities of life in His creation. These are evident (i.e. stars are different from plants and plants are different from animals). He uses this example to demonstrate that just like there are differences between various elements in the creation; there is also a difference between the human, natural body and the glorious, resurrected body.

He explains the differences between natural and spiritual (God creates both).

- Earthly body is perishable (decays); dishonorable (dies); weak (physically and morally).

- Spiritual body is imperishable (not subject to change or decomposition); glorious (no death); powerful (see the power of the angels – power over armies, nature, wisdom, space, time).

Paul says that like the seed is transformed into the flower, the natural body will be transformed into the spiritual body at the resurrection.

1. Why this is so

> Vs. 45-49 – So also it is written, "The first man, Adam, became a living soul." The last Adam became a life-giving spirit. However, the spiritual is not first, but the natural; then the spiritual. The first man is from the earth, earthy; the second man is from heaven. As is the earthy, so also are those who are earthy; and as is the heavenly, so also are those who are heavenly. Just as we have borne the image of the earthy, we will also bear the image of the heavenly.

Why do our natural bodies die and spiritual ones live? Our natural bodies are like this because we share in Adam's nature (human beings).

We will be changed into spiritual bodies because of our relationship with Jesus Christ. Just as our natural bodies resemble Adam because we are born of the flesh, our spiritual bodies will resemble Christ because we are born again in water and Spirit.

The great reward is that we will possess the glorious body similar to Christ's when He ascended into heaven after His resurrection.

2. How and when this change will take place

> Vs. 50-57 – Now I say this, brethren, that flesh and blood cannot inherit the kingdom of God; nor does the perishable inherit the imperishable. Behold, I tell you a mystery; we will not all sleep, but we will all be changed, in a moment, in the twinkling of an eye, at the last trumpet; for the trumpet will sound, and the dead will be raised imperishable, and we will be changed. For this perishable must put on the imperishable, and this mortal must put on immortality. But when this perishable will have put on the imperishable, and this mortal will have put on the immortality, then will come about the saying that is written, "death is swallowed up in the victory. O death, where is your victory? O death, where is your sting?" The sting of death is sin, and the power of sin is the law; but thanks be to God, who gives us the victory through our Lord Jesus Christ.

We cannot resurrect ourselves. Only those who share in Christ's death and resurrection through repentance and baptism will share in His resurrection when He returns. We have to share Christ's nature if we want to experience His resurrection. A tomato seed cannot grow an apple tree. A non-believer (seed) cannot bloom into a glorious eternal body.

The final transformation will occur at the last trumpet when we will be changed into our glorious bodies in an instant. Those Christians who are dead will resurrect with glorious bodies. Those Christians alive at His coming will be transformed into glorious bodies in the twinkling of an eye. All resurrected believers will come together to be with Christ forever.

All this done to fulfill God's promise that one day death, that made its entry into the world through Adam's sin, would finally be eliminated through Jesus Christ.

No more death for three reasons:

1. Satan is defeated, he will no longer be able to tempt men (no repeats of the garden).

2. The price of sin is paid for (no more law).

3. Glorious bodies know good and evil, and have chosen good in Christ once and for all (no more sin exists).

Summary

Vs. 58 –Therefore, my beloved brethren, be steadfast, immovable, always abounding in the work of the Lord, knowing that your toil is not in vain in the Lord.

A long passage about a complex subject, but essentially it boils down to three main ideas:

1. The resurrection of Jesus has happened and has been witnessed by hundreds of people, some of whom have documented what they have seen in the New Testament.

2. To doubt this fact leads to terrible consequences, the worst of which is the destruction of our own salvation. If Christ is not raised, then neither are we. If we do not believe that He was resurrected, we will be rejected by Him when He returns to raise the believers.

3. Our own resurrection will be the final act in the process of salvation that will see:

    a. The wicked destroyed (judged and punished).

    b. The believers equipped with glorious bodies fit for eternity.

    c. A final restoration of God and man in perfect harmony to last forever.

If these things be so, Paul urges them to persevere in the doing of good, knowing by faith that God will accomplish the wonderful things that He has promised when He returns.

BibleTalk.tv is an Internet Mission Work.

We provide textual Bible teaching material on our website and mobile apps for free. We enable churches and individuals all over the world to have access to high quality Bible materials for personal growth, group study or for teaching in their classes.

The goal of this mission work is to spread the gospel to the greatest number of people using the latest technology available. For the first time in history it is becoming possible to preach the gospel to the entire world at once. BibleTalk.tv is an effort to preach the gospel to all nations every day until Jesus returns.

The Choctaw Church of Christ in Oklahoma City is the sponsoring congregation for this work and provides the oversight for the BibleTalk ministry team. If you would like information on how you can support this ministry, please go to the link provided below.

bibletalk.tv/support

Made in the USA
Monee, IL
07 June 2023

35395318R00118